To: Joshua and Sandra

It was great to meet u

Share a dream with you

Brown

A TASTE OF ME

Devouring Powerful Words To Accomplish A Dream

by
Heavenly Brown

Bloomington, IN Milton Keynes, UK

authorHOUSE®

AuthorHouse™
1663 Liberty Drive, Suite 200
Bloomington, IN 47403
www.authorhouse.com
Phone: 1-800-839-8640

AuthorHouse™ UK Ltd.
500 Avebury Boulevard
Central Milton Keynes, MK9 2BE
www.authorhouse.co.uk
Phone: 08001974150

First published by AuthorHouse 1/25/2007

ISBN: 978-1-4259-7047-5 (sc)

Printed in the United States of America
Bloomington, Indiana

This book is printed on acid-free paper.

Library of Congress Control Number: 2006909108

Welcome to the beginning of this story.

It is a half-cup of fact
and a pound of fiction.

It is a reflection and interpretation of the self.

It is you and me

on different ends of the earth,
with the same feelings and fears.

It is a pinch of love and a dash of despair.

It is devouring powerful words to accomplish a dream.

It is always wanting to
and finally doing something about it.

To My Mother,
Diana

One day the little girl awakened to see her mother
Down on her knees
Praying in the dark
The woman sobbed and asked
"Please help me take care of my children"

As the youngster pretended to be asleep
She listened and watched
It was the first day she realized
No matter what
Her mother cared

Author's Note

This is a narrative with lots of flavor. For the purpose of this book, flavor means there is a variety of writing styles, talents, stories and issues that will become prominent in the reading. When I say "the restrictions in literature bind me," keep in mind that I consider my style nontraditional and have put myself in first, second and third person intentionally. I have also included a half-cup of fact and a pound of fiction, while respectfully changing the names of some individuals. To those who venture to taste this, I would like you to tuck away a feeling of accomplishment on the back of your palate. As you swallow an epicurean delight, digest the power of words and be inspired to do something you always wanted to do. Think positive! Surround yourself with everything that will make you try. Then break free and realize you are finally taking steps to do something about your own convictions. As you make it to the finish, recognize that success comes in all sorts of packages.

CONTENTS

1

SOMETHING OUT OF NOTHING

Today is as good a day as any to give you a taste of me. I am an amateur with no real publishing skills—who wants to follow through and finish something that I started but never finished.

After years of telling myself that I am going to write this book, I am finally ready to put the words down on fastened sheets of paper and keep them there. No more writing a paragraph or two and throwing it away. No more days of erasing creativity and asking *those who don't know exactly what I am trying to say,* to edit my words into what becomes their version of my story.

In other words,
I have something to say!
And with my own sense of literary flavor,
I am ready to make something out of nothing!

So I start mixing, cutting, filling, squeezing, peeling and combining and it has my nervous system in synapse. From one end of the spectrum to the next, I am reveling in unknown territory where I become susceptible to the effects of criticism. My heart rate is already speeding up and with every ended sentence and test of oil, I know there is a script lurking inside of me that has not been set forth.

My friends and colleagues say I am in the wrong profession. I work many hours caring for the sick and injured and at the end of a long day, I kick off my shoes, sip on that glass of satisfying wine, write feverishly and tend to agree with those who favor me. Line after line, I fantasize in the hinterlands of my imagination but resist putting myself in a place where I know I belong.

This is all too familiar and should be no surprise to any one of us. We become a certain epoch and think adventure is a bold action left to the spirit of our youthful past. We become complacent, ignore the discovery of change and get stuck in a pattern of life that becomes our pacemaker.

Should I patronize and make this a little more real for you? Can I really create a beginning, find my way through the heart of it and come to an ending; or am I sifting through contaminated flour that has been sitting in the pantry a year past its' expiration date? Good or bad: Go beyond that feeling of a refined grain slipping through your fingers. As the dough forms, grab onto your heart, rip it out, and set it directly in front of you. As you begin to knead, realize the beautiful hollow mass which fits into the palm of your hand—is being restored.

Go ahead—make something out of nothing and express your inner self. Start that slow sweet move in the conduction system. Kiss the sinus node with electrical spark and watch it jolt your understanding 60 to 100 times a minute. With every pulsation there is an explosion and a domino effect making you aware that you are alive and being taken. Start your inter-nodal dance and capture all that is in your path. Wear yourself out on the feeling and make sure you close your eyes so tight, that they are wide open. Hit the atrioventricular node and just for a while, let it take you over at 40 to 60 continuous beats. Slide down the Bundle of His, and as your breath is being taken away, deny this most erotic dance and try to choose where to go from here. Should you move more towards the left or right? Should you command yourself to stop or to try? Should you lie back and let impulse take over at a slower propulsive pace or should you allow your life to start over once again?

In this moment of blithe and bliss you are thinking, thinking, thinking. The world will not go on standby for you and all the voices are calling out to you. The sky says abstain while the wind says attain. As you add water to the mix, we are now kneading at 15 to 40 slow beats. It is clear that we are struggling to go in any direction and make our own decisions. All of this excitement is turning into chaos, confusion, missed opportunity and fear. The doubt is taking us further and further away from realizing our action potential and there may be error in the mixture of the flour and water.

Then my words confronted me. *"So look at your heart now! As you hold it in your hand, is it what you intended it to be or is it a model of unbaked dough?"* As these kinds of thoughts enter my mind ask yourself, "Where are you in the dance that gives rhythm to your heart and what do your words want to say about it?"

Personally, I am in the quiet before the storm and certain ignorance's, pressures and contaminants leave me unable or unwilling to take the next step. Truthfully, I want to say that I am manipulated. I want to say all of "this and that" keeps me from the finish and has not allowed me to come face to face with the persons inside of me called:

Wit,
Demon,
Reticence,
Creativity,
and
Personality.

You see, they are all a part of me—my Allies—who insist that I pay more attention to them and their words. Thus, with each passing day, they are the "we" and "I" and "them" that has rallied to get me here— and that is how this story begins.

Chapter 1

BREAKING THE RULES

As you picture me, I am still in a frame of mind that exists only in the imagination. I twist and turn in the patio chair, while the early morning air leaves me leaning towards a pleasant aroma. I smile in that state of abstraction and remember how the smell of Sister's cooking was strong enough to wake me out of this kind of deep sleep and compelling enough to have me up and securing a place at the kitchen table.

In a moment, I would gather my utensils, listen to the hypnotic sizzle from the pan and watch her hands roll, pat, form and deliver the perfect meal. Thirty years ago—PERFECT— did not mean you threw salt and spices and yelled BAM! It meant you came into my world and picked up and ate anything you dropped. It meant you sucked your fingers, licked your plate and found a reason to have seconds.

How could you have good table manners when the food was so good? It was better than delicious and the way you ate it had no place in the books of etiquette. Don't you remember?

> Hey, forget where the glasses and
> napkins go and let's eat! Oh no, the
> Lord's Prayer. *Mother* is not around,
> can't we shorten it? I say seeing is
> believing and when I finish with this
> plate, the Holy Spirit will know that
> I am more than grateful. Ok, I can
> see that no one is going to agree with
> my idea of AMEN, so let us just hurry
> up—I really want to put this gift where
> it belongs.

> What now? You want me to wait
> another minute for the rest of the world
> to be served? This is scandalous and
> one of those times when I think having
> a much smaller family would be an
> advantage. My goodness, it is sitting
> right in front of me—and the smell of
> all that greatness is driving me crazy.

> I protest! And with every whiff, I feel
> myself getting ready to break the rules
> and beat the fork handle into the table.

I do not want my food to get cold and
... Finally! We have the all-clear signal
and I can dig in. I waited so long that
I can not slow down and I can't get all
this exquisite cuisine into my mouth at
one time. With every bite, the juice is
dripping and splattering everywhere—I
am into it now.

Who cares about the drama taking
place around the table! My tongue is in
tune with magnificent flavors and has
a catchall action that feels the various
textures swirling around on it. Nothing
is wrong now, as I tell myself "this is so
good."

OH NO, COME ON! Why interrupt
me to wipe the remnants of good food
off of my face? Don't hurt my feelings
and say that I look like I have no table
manners. I am a kid and all I want to
do is show my appreciation—for your
hard work.

Decades later in my own culinary sphere, there were
plenty of efforts to build from my mother's talents and
replicate Sister's special dishes. Five days a week, I was
a taste short—and you should have seen me referencing
those old cookbooks. I mixed and stirred as instructed

but still ended up dropping a dime and calling home for assistance.

No surprises. Sister had a set of conventions that were her very own. There was no looking in a book and using fixed measurements. There were only delicious outcomes and comfort guided by her saying, "You use a little bit of *this* and a little bit of *that*." Looking at myself now, this is where I find myself in my kitchen of printed works. I am holding a pen and I am assembling a dish where no words, subject, form, style or color has to be excluded from the samples served. With "a little bit of *this* and a little bit of *that*," you can see me, read me, and hear the thoughts behind my words.

Some days those words are colored black and when I turn them over to someone else they become white. Other days when my words are white and black or green and red and brown, the grammar is not quite right and imperfect is impolite. Attention to revision and the results of the echocardiogram (EKG) imply—I insisted on creating in a system that was not working for me.

Can you hear me? The restrictions in literature bind me and take away from the nutrients in my thoughts. They perplex me and after burning the midnight oil on a journey that is more than the flavor of our existence, I awake knowing that it is time to stop reheating and microwaving the same dish. It is time to stop destroying everything that I create and time to free myself from a straight jacket designed to hold someone like you or me back.

As I press start and let go of the old system, I am ready to let the writer put the words down and keep them there. As I am warming up to comfortable, I gesticulate the rules of syntax. I take years of fact and fiction and deliver it to you while I am away from home, out of my comfort zone and with you.

Purposely, I intend to put the other side of me in a very different place: where I can go back to the basics, take my face off, make plans to overcome my limitations, play with the possibilities, cover up in fraudulent fur or just decide to be me. Nothing in this story has to be true but at the same time it can be as real as that unforgettable meal that holds a person's interest from the first bite to the last.

So relax! With this venue that I am presenting, we can be in first, second or third person any time we wish. Be delighted, because we can concoct any type of filling as long as it makes a pie that is pleasing to you. In retrospect, I want you to taste me—and if it is good enough, I want you to ask for more.

Chapter 2 —

MONDAY DID COME

"OUT OF ORDER" and my life was not giving back anything for the change that was being put into it. I can still see them standing there as if I was an unreliable vending machine. They were using profanities, refusing to call the posted one-eight-hundred number for help and insisting on kicking and beating me down until I produced something. To produce means to generate something, to contribute and to follow through with delivery. All in all, I am not sure how much I could have provided back then but right now something tells me that I can yield much more.

It has been a long road and at first I truly believed there was not a thing in this life that I could do. As a child I invested most of my time in my thoughts instead of my education. People would say hello and I would walk past them and turn into the next fantasy. Reality only caught up to me in bits and pieces and as I fell deeper and deeper into a premier, I would suddenly find myself standing in the middle of a street in front of a car. The horn would be off-the-hook and the driver would be half-way out of the car calling me all kinds of deaf and dumb. At the time, I could not be scared. I had too much to process and I needed to figure out what just happened. Really, who would think that this habit would begin to put me in harm's way!

Then my face said hello to a telephone pole and some days later, I walked into the path of an elderly women who cursed me as her frail body landed on a set of marble steps. I snapped out of it, said "sorry" and reached down and picked up the lady's cane. My two friends, who made way for the woman, just stared at me with their mouths open. I said to the lady, "I did not see you," but what good did that do? Once the lady was stable on her feet, she put some bad words on me and almost landed her cane upside my head.

"Wow" is all that I could tell myself—and as I committed more to reality, I had a hard time figuring out what I could do. My high school graduation was in the near future and I was the only one who knew that I was not prepared for the next step in life. I could not figure the north from the south and math was a detriment. Yet, after the ceremony, I made decisions, choices and had G-O-A-L-S. They seemed attainable; but when countless others told me where my intellectualism started and ended, I lost my confidence. As my situation became more complicated, I realized I had to stop being at the mercy of others and needed to start believing in me.

I took steps to teach myself some things and gathered every bit of my unfinished letters and incomplete journals to write this book. Although I had never done it before, I was going to say exactly what I wanted to say, exactly how I wanted to say it. Of course, I was going to finish the thing, publish it and then the "BUT!" It was a word that suggested doubt, caution and conditions. It was a word that meant someone convinced the crowd outside the vending machine, that I could not be fixed. They were frustrated—and I could not be optimistic. I watched my words and my work, politely and slightly start to change into someone else's meaning and concept.

Then, *Monday did come*—and that day was very different from all the rest. **Creativity** fell out of me and found itself in the kitchen baking bread. **Tuesday**, the doctor called with good news and said there was no ectopy in **Reticence's** heart. On **Wednesday**, the surface side of me seemed just right. **Personality** managed a smile in the light of adversity and I remembered my dream—it was another chance and a notion of success. Then **Demon** looked in the mirror on **Thursday** and caught sight of a stranger mouthing something to me. I dared to take a look at the reflecting image and saw two persons standing several meters away from one another. They were unknown to me and on **Friday** they met in a face-off; I thought I was dead as a result of an internal struggle. At the end of the count, **Wit** showed up on **Saturday** and told me that I was alive and truly committed to finishing what I started. Wholehearted and pledged, I sighed with relief, put myself in the best chair on my patio and rested. As **Sunday** began, the sun rolled over a cloud, propped itself on the edge of the sky, and told me it wanted "A TASTE OF ME."

At that point, my heart was lulled back into existence and I realized there was enough electricity left inside of me to knead another day. There was hope instead of hopelessness and enough current to learn how to understand the combination of life's positive and negative charges.

"Lubb-Dubb" and there was:
Enough to make my own decisions,
Enough to try regardless,
Enough to be true to myself,
Enough to be dedicated,
Enough to be free of my insecurities,
Enough to be literary,
Enough to believe,
Enough to choose a path and
Enough to complete the dance
that gives rhythm to my heart.

Chapter 3 —

39,000 FEET

American, Delta, Continental, ATA—I could still get away from doing this. I could buy a ticket and be like the woman inside me who gets up in the middle of the night to drive nowhere. I sit straight up in the aisle seat. I push the button and the flight attendant appears at A3. "I would like a cup of coffee please. Black with no sugar…No, on the other hand let's change that today. Add cream and sugar."

It is a day of nerves and I need something to get me going. There is numbness in the center of my back and my pen is stiff. I can finally travel freely; yet, I am 39,000 feet above the rules and feel worried about the landing.

Eyes to the right and reality to the left; the coffee is hot and strong and you are sitting next to me. I feel your eyes on me and wonder if you need to get by. After moments of silence, I tuck that empty cup in the seat sleeve in front of me and tell myself "all I have are words, and they can be configured whenever I want, wherever I want and however I want."

I start to forge ahead and just when I am about to lift off the page, the individual beside me decides to take interest. I was hoping to relay nonverbal messages of "NOT NOW" but conversation pursued and there was reception and response.

This person wanted to surf and get caught up in social dialogue. He wanted to know where I was from and what I did for a living. It was a normal sequence until he wanted to know something too real about "ME." In a moment I thought, "Only if you knew." Then I looked into your eyes and was interlaced and inventing the "SHE" that would be easy for you and him to relate to.

As I was speaking, my inner voice started to interfere and give me turbulence. It wanted to know what I was doing. It wanted to know why I always felt like I needed to be a fairytale that fits in. Then I stopped in the middle of the next sentence and excused myself. I walked the long narrow path of the 727 and was sure to lock the bathroom door behind me. I turned on the water in the sink and tried to figure out what I was doing. I stared at the transparent liquid until I felt it running inside of me. I was fixed—until **Wit** figured out that it is not a matter of fitting in but a matter of feeling comfortable with who you are and what you are.

I am my own barrier. I put up the blockades. I say can't instead of can. I believed them when they said I was ugly. I thought I was unworthy. I doubted my accomplishments and became that strange shooter questioning and figuring, going back and forth, only to move on to the next year in my life without rhyme or reason.

I suddenly heard the captain turn on the seat belt sign and I knew I had been in that small airplane space for way too long. I wiped my face and headed back to A3. The flight attendant announced that we were in descent and I knew there was no more time to find ways to escape.

I gathered my papers and bags and the person beside me said that it was wonderful meeting me. I smiled with respect and stepped out into the crowd. I walked briskly and looked for the signs that said Ground Transportation and Extended Parking. As I left the concourse I thought about my experience and shuddered knowing I was still that long-lost teenager who was described "different" by every teacher.

Pubescent and vain, I sat in a parent-teacher conference and dared anyone to get me right. It was a sophisticated game of chess and I got tired of winning. Check! And as I slowly eliminated the pieces on the board, I succeeded in writing simple pieces of poetry that swallowed up my energy and produced strategic animations that the world could acknowledge, accept and understand.

Idling back and forth into what was and what is, I could not stop thinking about that person on the plane. Frankly, I did not want to expose any part of what lies beneath my surface; I wanted that stranger to be an internal harmony that never forced me to take a good look at myself. In fact, when I was driving home, I thought I was ready to confront **Demon**. But in sixty seconds I was convinced that I never talked to anyone.

I told all of me that I had earned the man's favor, so I wiped the worry of another lie from my brow, reached over the dash and readjusted my rearview mirror. I turned on the radio and in a metrical composition, the lyrist within my imagination set the record straight.

———

It is not another lie
Because I am up in the sky
  sitting next to a weird white guy
For two hours and fifty-four minutes
He eats, he reads, he looks, and he listens

He's buckled up and following all safety tips
While drinking and making noises on the cup
  with his bottom lip
Dr. Pepper I do believe
Probably some cat named Steve

Oh my, what a weird guy

Dressed in a long out-of-date shirt
He's not the type to wink an eye and flirt
Not too much to say
Because he knows I am much too busy
  to converse on this day

I am buried in my thoughts and trying not to cry
This guy really does not need to know
  the reasons why
Seat B3 and in the clouds he did see
The turmoil sitting like stuffing right inside of me

Maybe I am really the weird guy

We are up in the sky and much time has passed
Lurking around in my own mind at last
Following this flight, I will wish him goodnight
And find a way to make our encounter a delight

Flight 1582 and that is all I could write
So farewell to what has become
  another fantasy night

**UP IN THE SKY NEXT TO A
WEIRD WHITE GUY**

Chapter 4

YOU DON'T KNOW ME

I did not hear the alarm that was to wake me but I heard the person on the radio, who said:

> Affable confidants of tomorrow, let us start over and make things right. You don't know me, and it would only be right to step away from the wall and face you. I am the entity who is trembling inside because no one knows this "E STORY" but me. I come from a life where everything in it and about it was fact and fiction. The secrets were about more than airing dirty laundry. They were about a false family and everyone involved becoming secrets themselves.

I was a little out of sorts and I asked out loud, "Who is that?" Of course no one answered. Then I heard:

First we were rich; then we were poor. All of the children (six in total) lived in a small, two-story, three-bedroom, one-bath house. Things were perfect until:

The priest gave me the
impression that you had
to be a certain religion
for God to love you;

I came home to Dad
beating Mom in front of
numerous audiences;

The typing teacher
tarnished me;

There was someone
missing at the dinner
table;

A couple of neighbors
tried to buy me for
services;

Taking a life was easier
than keeping it in
shame;

Attraction became a fear;

The one who meant the
most to me was only half
of me;

The rest of the family
started showing up;

My history was not my
history anymore and
there were no roots to
home, environment or
culture.

That's crazy! Who would be putting a buzz session on
the radio this early? I was getting restless, but the person
continued talking:

I was lost. Therefore, finding a way to a real
family and a better life meant going to the places
that lived as fantasies inside me. Every year, I
stood up in my class and told everyone I had
been on vacation in a place that would make
even the affluent envious. With nappy hair and
ashy brown skin, I stood with confidence and
conviction in my voice and made the world what I
wanted it to be.

Fearless, I told myself that everything was real
and I was prepared for the audience and teacher to
question and call me a prevaricator. As the high-

end listened, the bases were all covered to include hotel, restaurants and street names. Certainly, in my position, price was avoided but every sight had a major attraction and I was right there admiring it and finding adjectives to make it as awesome as it was supposed to be. The sordid, incapable child turned sugar, water and fruit into a tantalizing sweet and handed out complimentary candy, pens and brochures. She shared the Atlas experience with certainty and convinced her peers that each summer getaway had to be real because there was memorabilia to prove it.

Upon high school graduation, I thought I had to decide between "dying"—which meant staying at home in an unfavorable environment and "living"—which meant leaving and trying to get along in a world that promoted itself to be more than just one neighborhood and more than one way of life. Desperate and seeking a way to make my profound lies become truths, I signed myself over to this society's Uncle Sam. As fantasy became spotlights of reality, he unveiled a shy, naïve child, provided for her basic needs, surrounded her with rules and regulations, with people better off and worse off, and allowed her to fall but so far. Slowly the pieces to the puzzle started to fit into place and:

There were no longer reasons to ask myself WHY ME and all of the reasons to answer WHY NOT ME.

Pondering in a distinct space, I realized that I had always felt like an orphaned child without a family. "Why me" was a big question then, but what difference did that make right now? I was past that first day of trying to tell my mother that she did not know me and over the last day of trying to convince her—we were not a family.

Ok, that was it! I heard too much from the guest on the morning talk show and reached over to hit the off button. It was a simple task but I somehow missed the mark. I attempted to try again, when I opened my eyes to blinking green numbers and a red light. Slowly the rays broke at a twenty degree angle and hinted that someone had gained access to a moment in my past—that seemed impossible to forget. I started to scream, "You are a plagiarist tampering with the thoughts of my unconscious mind." I covered my head with a pillow and as I began to slowly take into account what was really happening, the walls in my room shifted into a box and I remembered my old house.

There I was sitting on the third step from the bottom of the staircase. My older brother had just slapped me in the head and ripped my hat off. As he threw it to the floor, he laughed and taunted me. Oh how I wished for strength to knock that cruel boy out! One-two, one-two is all I could think of—but then I heard my only retaliation, "You Asshole!" There was one second of silence, which was followed by another one of Big Brother's ridiculing laughs and a fraudulent call out to our mother, "Your daughter is cursing!"

I could hear Mrs. Brown stirring that pot and screaming out to us that we were a family and should not be fighting. I could not help but wonder why she would say something like that when, as of late, all I ever witnessed or experienced was of a combative and warlike nature. I bellowed out, "We are not a family!"

Just like that, the God-fearing woman was suddenly standing in front of me and challenging, "What did you say?" I could hardly get the words out. "This ain't no family." Three decibels above normal, Mother reiterated that she did not ever want to hear me say that again!

> Minds-eye! A family is supposed to be a unit closely related through love and a common ancestor. How could this be a family, when genealogy wasn't even an important factor in this place? Dad did not talk about his dad, Mom did not talk about her mom and most importantly — questions about their lineage were forbidden.

I gathered my attitude and decided to let every thought I had reveal themselves. Surely mother was forgetting something!

> Our roots had not been planted deep into the soil and our family tree held only new leaves with many structural defects. Essential elements were

desperately needed in our household! Breaking down: And the only constituents that my parents seemed concerned with—were those tied up in getting an education and learning how to live and survive in what was then a white world.

Tears rolled down my face and in that moment, nothing else mattered. Things did not make sense and I could not help but wonder "Why me and why was I put here?"

Was I here ***to be***:
> Loved one minute and hated the next?
> Up and then down?
> With people in the physical state but
>   somewhere else in my mind?
> Able to tell the truth, but not be allowed to?
> Quiet, but have so much to say?

Was I there ***to have:***
> Two parents and then one?
> Brothers and sisters, yet feel like
>   I was not a part of them?
> Someone say they knew me—when there was
>   no possible way they could?

Was I here ***to think:***
> I was the cause of my family's problems,
>   when I really was not?
> A child should stay in a child's place
>   no matter what?

Was I here **to learn**:
>That the same people could fight—and
>>somehow love one another, again and again?
>That you can predict anything but
>>nothing is certain?
>That I may never understand?

I stood there spinning with revolving emotions. I tried to land on stop but my Allies that I refer to in this story as "We"—encouraged a child to let a parent know that something was wrong. It took seconds, minutes, hours, days, and years to get up enough courage to talk back. My throat developed a sudden lump of soreness. It was dry and hard and everything about it told me that it was in lockdown. Finally, the arch of my palate-to the glottis-to the esophagus relaxed, and I could speak past the fear.

"This ain't no family! Everyone around here is cruel and crazy. You don't have to do a thing wrong but guess what? You end up in the middle of a fight where you get smacked around, teased, beat up and tortured!" I was screaming the words by now. "You don't know me and this definitely ain't no..." I could see her hand in motion. It crossed my face and echoed like a clap in an empty room. I stopped in mid-sentence; I could hear that someone was slapped, but I did not feel a thing. I looked straight into Mother's eyes and all of my tears were gone.

There was nothing left to say because she, he, them, they, you and me did not know who I was or what I was about to become.

Chapter 5—

FACADE

I beat the odds. I have experienced two graduations after leaving home and signing off from my controversial Uncle, who some time ago, ordered pride to stand up in me. As I twisted and turned in a long sleep, I heard the echoes of my own voice telling me to rejoice. I stood at attention and as someone was pinning metals of honor to my sleeves the orator said "You have reason to live, love, laugh, sing and smile!" I had no idea of my expression but before I could carry on, I had to repeat the words that were being said. Then, I no longer had to convince myself or those standing before me that I had what it took to learn and acquire knowledge!

Indeed—investigators of truth and principle would say I now had the world in my hands and it would be offering itself to me in countless ways. They would argue that I was no longer constrained and that education levels the playing field. They would put forth that my performance in this F-R-E-E society gives me liberty, legitimacy and legacy. They would claim that my life had fallen into place and that I was wise enough to know:

Facts are real and evident by what has been accomplished.

Fiction is not real; it is only what is perceived or what is made up in a persons mind.

Façade is the superficial appearance of SHE, HE, THEM, THEY YOU and ME.

So why, after all of this, am I still missing from the world? Why do all of my Allies on the inside—keep walking away? Why do we continue to present as a stranger in every aspect of our life? Why can't we keep my words on paper and begin? Why can't we start somewhere instead of finding ourselves nowhere?

Then one day I took it upon myself to look back. I remembered three little girls being told, "You have each other...therefore, you don't need much else in the way of friendships." They were sisters and every parent's prodigy destined to be closer than most, better than the rest and self-acclaimed to fame.

In the ambiance, joy and laughter sometimes filled the dead space in their home. In the backdrop: There were tugs of war, sibling rivalries, screams of envy, fights for individuality and the many things that children manage to do to have fun and keep themselves busy.

"One-H, Two-V and Three-K" sang and danced in their studio home. V would put out the belly moves and belt out the sounds, while K put on the heels and invented breast implants long before they were a novelty. H did not have much rhythm, so she served up hors-d'oeuvres from her Easy-Bake Oven and filled in as a back up.

Accordingly, they were celebrities in their own minds and nothing but stateliness in the trenches of the ghetto. Locked in after dark and peering at the freedoms that others seemed to have, they began opening with nights of fireworks in their neighbor's back yard. The firecrackers would sound off consecutively and the old guy next door would come running out with his hat, coke-bottle glasses, shot gun and choice words (*ok, mother fu----'s*). This guy was definitely a partier and you had better believe it when I say, there was plenty more where that came from.

Ha! Ha! Ha! And now it was time to open up the windows to the back room and put on a fashion show that would knock the socks off the crowd. It was a warm summer night and a perfect time; Mother was away *"earning the bacon"* and the three blood-linked Nubians were in alliance to do something good for their community.

The audience was *raining men*. Young, old and the like—they were attentive and most definitely awestruck. The music was blasting and on the rooftop above, the lights were bright. From a *flicker to a flame*, mother's wigs, makeup, brassieres, panties, stockings, and shoes were made public on the bodies of the preadolescents.

Songs of the present and legs up for the future: These African beauties were *baby-oiling* it, wearing gloves of gold and making demos for the thong-song long before it was ever thought of. They were adorning the Indian head wear and flashing jewelry and makeup that put ladies in the '20s and '30s to shame and the women of the '60s and '70s on the map.

Living it up and enjoying the gathering and acceptance of the crowd was all too real. It was "Epic Hollywood" and a visual art that was laid to rest when the downstairs door cracked open. Uh-oh! The voice of authority raced up the stairwell and into a blackened room of fast pulses—sleeping in adult costumes and praying under the covers of innocence.

The curtain was down, the crowd was still lurking and the children had to break into theater mode with fake yawns and stretches of daily wear and tear. Slowly but surely, someone was pulling a fast one but mother was already informed by her senses and would have her babies out of façade sooner than later.

Simply stated…Those playful, superficial appearances started right there in child's play. We were descendents

dreaming while the western hemisphere was interpreting.
For those who needed to take the next step but could not
talk about it or control it, FACADE is—

———

A smile in the depth of pain,
A laugh in the shadow of fear,
And a lie in the middle of truth.

You can build it or be it.
You can avoid it or become it.
You can see it or erase it.

It is portraying yourself at work;
While concealing yourself inside.

It is constructing the family you always wanted;
And refusing to reckon with the family you have.

It is a direct confrontation,
That is trying to distinguish you
  from your outer-self.

It is a subversive Uncle.
It is being told that you are equal,
  even when you look different.

It is being mistreated
  despite your accomplishments;
And thinking—you are really free.

It is touching "yourself"
And imagining it is someone else.

It is eating a food you do not like
And convincing others that you savored it.

It is being multicolored
And choosing which culture is most important.

It is witnessing hate that is mistaken for love.
Then claiming love in the twilight of hate.

It is fact in the middle of fiction,
Fiction in the midst of truth and—
Creating a story that includes you.

FACADE

Chapter 6—

DISCOVERING WHAT WORKS

The gossip was surrounding me and I heard them say, "It can't be true that the tiny baby was born in a basement." Everyone said I made it up—but on a cold night I remembered how my older brother and I were residing in the bottom of an old house.

Sometimes I could hear Romey whimpering but I was too young to do anything about our situation. I am sure that I sensed something was wrong—but with my tears all dried up and a baby blanket trailing behind me, I played and slept on the padded section of a cement floor. In the image of a more grandeur moment, this big furry dog took responsibility for me. She stayed at my side and calmed me and her puppies—making a pact for us all to stay warm.

Every once in a while I could feel quivers from the sounds in the earth above me. And like magic, the dungeon doors would open slowly and allow my brother and me into the light. I still go blank on some of the details but once we made it to the top of the stairs, the stern woman in the castle gave us a bite to eat. "Hurry it up," she would say and then as soon as the odd odor that consumed us started to smell like fresh air—we were returned to our living space as quickly as we had arrived.

Facts were not what people wanted to hear; Romey held on to the door and had to be pushed back into the basement. He could not comprehend what was happening to him but through it all, his sister was welcomed back by her four legged companions who kissed the crumbs off of her face and settled her down into the warmth of their litter. It was all true but when I told the nun I was born in a basement with dogs, she credited my big imagination and told me if I continued in such a manner I would land in the fires of hell.

I was assigned a simple class project: I was told to come up to the front of the class, say I was born in a "hospital" and report something nice about my family. Hesitant, I started out with that L-I-E and it was taken to be true. Then again, it was the way everything in my life seemed to work. I was told not to ever lie, attempted to tell the whole truth and got popped. "Careful" is what the rest of me would say. So, **Wit** discovered what worked! If the nun asked if everything was alright at home, I would tell her it was good—even if it wasn't. I said I was happy, even when I was sad. If the typing teacher had a different lesson plan on non-typing days, I was typing. Thus, the taste buds on the back of my tongue became painful sins—which remained hidden as long as I kept my mouth shut.

Life moved along and as I settled into becoming a half-cup of fact and a pound of fiction; Big Brother (now a man wrestling with his own ghost) asked me if I remembered the old basement. Stunned, I reached deep within myself, calmly filled in the blanks and assured him that his recent memory was not a hallucination. It was repressed truth put on a different end of the earth by a boy, and excluded by a man. "I don't believe this!" And my gut told me, "That's where those supportive characters inside of you were born." I stood very still and again I heard something say, "That's right, your Allies were born in the bowels of that dark basement and now they want to be delivered into a new day."

At that very moment, I opened my mouth—then closed it. I realized I was still operating on what worked for those around me and was wondering if I could now reclaim truth. I told myself, "You were not always a fictional character that had to become tangible for people to believe you!" A blue cloud suddenly showed itself and the "We" inside of me—the Allies— suddenly became unsettled. They wanted to open their mouth, become literary and talk about those distinctive flavors that defined them and made them more prominent in my life.

Now don't be confused with the message being delivered here. I am not attempting to "clean out my closet." Come on, you must have heard that term by now. If not, you can easily be updated while you are sitting in your vehicle at a red light. The car on Ritalin pulls up beside you nice and slow. It puts its engine in neutral, looks at you and instantly acts like a transcending vibrator that *spits* rap out to you real hard. In the middle of the *spew*, Eminem says, "I'm sorry momma—I never meant to hurt you—I never meant to make you cry—but tonight I'm cleaning out my closet!"

That is not what this is about. "A TASTE OF ME" is a conglomeration of different life aspects, experiences and ideas, which determine my literary flavor and style. It is the sizzle in a pan and a memory in your mouth. It is devouring powerful words to accomplish a dream. It is realizing the restrictions that I placed upon myself. It is discovering love just might be the root of a magnificent meal. It is you and I on different ends of the earth and finally getting past what has prevented us from being where we wanted to be in the first place. It is taking the next step in completing something. It is countering the passive and keeping an individual's medium of expression from disappearing. It is gaining enough courage to let the inside of me be heard.

Hence, it is us developing a millionaire mind, investing in ourselves and choosing better outcomes. It is forgiving those that have done the unthinkable and never giving up on T-R-U-T-H, hope or desire. It is teaching each other instead of turning our backs on one another. It is finding a way and realizing everything at the top, has the potential to find it self floating among the unfortunate things on the bottom. It is living the life I was meant to lead and understanding that all I must do today is hold on to who I really am.

In truth, it is time to set facade aside.
It is time to do more than what just works.
It is time to want, confront and try to:
Make it, describe it and inscribe it
Until there is attainment of an epicurean delight.

Yummy! It may sound far-fetched, but let's find personal meaning in this narrative; make admissions of fact and fiction in one big sentence; add truth, humor and fun to the menu; run words on and on until the listed courses are complete. Then, let's see what happens—especially when one includes those subliminal seasonings of intention, purpose, cause and depth.

Chapter 7

ADMIT

So I acknowledge it all and swallowed my whole life. As I began my testimony, it was an uninterrupted sentence that moved from lower to higher concentrations of wisdom in my head. As the pressure and temperature rose within me, letters moved past the sutures in my head and seeped out these words onto my pillow.

> "Admit it and avow that everybody
> wants to be somebody somehow, which
> means that anything we choose to be
> or do, could be a matter of personalized
> significance, leading to an inward
> burst, ending in an impulse, taking

one step or two, then growing up into
who you call you, happy or not this
far you have come, listening to music
at the beat of your own drum, can
not tell you what to play, the choice
is yours each and everyday, no time
for an ending point, just life carried
on in a skeletal joint, connecting and
fearing so much time could be lost,
how much did the waste cost, in days
and seasons and plenty of reasons,
inner spirit to listen to, may be the best
friend inside of you, good intentions,
poised for retention, all words and issues
worth a mention, hearing and feeling,
wanting and waiting, leading to the
products of creation, no summation
just information, about the temptation
of sedation, some things misleading,
the mind swallowing and needing,
questions in the hemisphere, answer
upon answer except right here, vowing
to commit, then exiting without it,
wondering how they did it, changing
places, leaving no traces, welcoming new
faces, can't escape polarity, facing self
with sincerity, admit now to the who

in you, countdown from cue to cue, in
good spirit, analyzed thought, suddenly
caught, nothing brought, in and out
of the new year, for thyself wanting to
care, more than a name and a number,
definite smiles of wonder, capsized
every other day, no hesitance to wink
and play, it is part of the intimacy, all
aboard for curiosity, where is the fear
in being alone, must be tiptoeing in the
danger zone, animals more safe than a
non-trusting face, attracted to he and
she, choice of intimacy up to me, in the
best love affair, we all say we care but
it has always been that of red-colored
hair, selling out and selling in, food
for thought, family and kin, denial
approached slowly, nothing afforded
above or below me, suddenly breaking in
and saying I can, toast to healthcare any
area to dare, building a different place to
compare, seeing the licks of politics and
knowing within, all will meet a good
or bad end, devastations of legislations,
unable to join congregations, keeping it
clean but not sticking to what it means,
leading the flock, increasing your stock,

closing off a mind, scared to see other
rights they may find, no rejection to
complexion, looking in a mirror at one's
own reflection, never getting it right
in years as a parent, seems as though
effort's nil and transparent, giving too
much and then too little, equilibrium
never found in the fiddle, hurt and
pain, love remain, never giving up on
the land, leaving it all in the almighty
hand, hope there is no mishap to the
rap, just humming and bumming and
then becoming, every night in the
wake, a word to discover, construct and
generate, contemplating the rights and
wrong of destined fate, mind goes on
and on in a continuous state, it is so
hazy some think I am crazy, turns out to
be amazing, in this fight, for attainment
of an epicurean delight, finally got it
right, sifting through a mind that dines,
taste the wines, smells the pines, no
easy answers on ways to admit—just
knowing it takes your heart to commit."

Then I opened my eyes and it seemed like my osmosis
dissolved into those elements that had accumulated
throughout my life.

Chapter 8—

NOTHING IS AS IT APPEARS

You know, nothing has to be as it appears. Our dreams can become more than thoughts. They can waver in and out and become schizophrenic delusions that we insert into our minds as real. Who knows? They could be many words, sentences and ideas swiftly moving along in a mind that is incapable of interrupting or stopping itself from expressing its various opinions. The words say this is fiction, but a theater surrounds the possibilities of our imagination with a grand audience, feeds a message into the gray and white matter of our emotions and suddenly—fiction is interpreted as fact, and fact is lost to fairytales.

No more stress or anxiety, because if nothing is as it appears, we have an outlet and the ability to turn any situation into a parable. "Lubb-dubb," and just as seasons change, I was finally awake! Again, I looked toward the clock but that which took me back in time did not exist. I was still gathered up in an awkward position in my lawn chair. I must have been there about ninety minutes cycling in and out of tabulated visions.

As I looked around, I noticed that the trees were swaying and the birds were searching for small pieces of wooden branches to complete their nests. I was cognizant now. My dogs were barking and chasing one another across the yard, as a couple wandered past the gate. I am sure I commanded a "shush" as the two of them continued in a slow stroll—holding hands, smiling, laughing and appearing to be content. They suddenly had my attention, as I noticed the warm feelings emanating from their scene of displayed affection.

He was a throbbing pulsation and she was a soft character ever so affected by light percussion. As they moved further away towards the lake that lies in the middle of a quiet community, he whispered something in her ear and the gestures of their lips moving toward one another caused me to think about those special persons that you and I have already tasted and shared our lives with.

In the beginning nothing is as it appears. Without reasoning, we are compelled to do something different to let the accompanying individual know they are like no other. Attraction spins the wheels of passion and drives

Personality to do something a little crazy. Maybe it is showing up with an oversized sign, asking for boxers instead of biscuits or ordering panties instead of pasta. Allurement is the bottom line and as we move past the enticing character; we realize there is a gravitational force, which sends a message that makes one feel naked under their coat.

Back in Philly, there was Fea, then Wiggins... and finally Chester! He was the aberration that made a young lady think about the adventures of being a woman. Blocks away you could smell him coming and there was no way you were going to let him see you sporting disheveled hair and shredded jeans. As the man drew closer, you could hear the ricochet of his name through the block and it seemed like there was not enough time to be prepared for his charisma and strong sweet way of making the worst day better.

Everyone said that when the right one comes along, you may feel overpowered by an unexplained force of numbness. In my case, every time Chester smiled or chuckled, I felt spears of delight in my stomach and blushed as the feeling moved all-the-way-up past my heart and into my head. "Oh what a feeling in the wilderness of the heart!"

Butterflies were bee-stings in youth and there was no way to prepare for those sharp-pointed moments. How did Lois Lane act when Superman was standing at her door? What did she say when the athlete swam in her eyes, left sweet tasting sparks on her lips, and smiled as he unveiled gifts of kryptonite that weakened her manner?

I asked myself, "Should I get up and get my pen to describe what I am feeling right now or should I keep watching the loving couple until their actions become the beginning and ending of my own experiences and proceedings?" Nothing is as it appears and just like a homemade dish, no story is exactly the same. We all know there may be similarities but the underlying differences lie within the fingerprints of a person's character and design.

Nothing is as it appears and that is why it may be the right time for me to try to interpret things as they really are for me and my entourage, which have already been introduced as my Allies: **Wit**, **Demon**, **Reticent**, **Creativity** and **Personality**.

Nothing is as it appears and as the "concentrations of two solutions" equalize, I will defeat my limitations and find a way to be comfortable going back to yesterday, coming back to today, and moving forward to forever.

Chapter 9

MY CARE AND DESPAIR

I am enjoying the thermosphere and as I stretch, I am feeling everything the written words cannot explain. Taken in by my surroundings and the love story unfolding right before me, I realize that I must put fear at a distance, accept the tremendous amount of energy that is being released and turn my attention to *you*. It may be perplexing but I drove over two thousand miles to get to this chapter in my life— and in my travels all I thought about was precious moments in a life, coming to terms with unavoidable fate that befalls a person, and *you*.

You are versatile and creative and I love that *you* are strong enough to stand up and say, "I am." *You* caught my attention on the first day that I laid eyes on *you*. Personification came before words and then your yearning

53

to learn and your appetite to discuss and take control, ordered me to employ a watchful eye. What else can I say, except that *you* are the one who makes me want to! *You* make me want to stand in front of the world and not be afraid of who I am and whatever I am.

You encourage me to put my words into prospective and ask the only God that I know to: let me climb high, then fall fast into the arms of wisdom; allow me to learn from that which leads to mountains of joy, hills of anguish or mounds of disappointment; protect me from my dreams because they may not be your dreams or their expectations.

You see the informal reflections of me that I like and it makes me want to be here without my customary covering. It makes me render to *you* that I do not want to live without trying, die as a coward, have my conscious referenced as a liar or be someone *you* have never known.

As the wind began to pick up, I turned back towards that couple and could see them kiss to infinity. I tried not to stare but as they broke into a run and then into a sudden stop in front of the water, I became fascinated and full.

**Eyes closed so tight, that they are wide open,
I bow my head and fall to my knees.**

My life flashes before me. It has been instant and abundant; it has encountered fun, adventure, thrill, chill, fear, care and many emotional ups and downs. With tears of joy and pain exuding themselves from the visible eye, I know at this very moment my biggest fear is to exist as a programmed mutation. Very few know me and I, like many others, have shied away in wonderment about how individuals of this genus can find it easy to distress, impair, enslave, ruse and offend one another.

People say they love you and then they take a peculiar turn and cut your soul in two. It is all in the principles of life, where half of what you had is left cold and the other warm. Sometimes it takes forever to merge this all-important part of you and I just wonder how anyone could intentionally dash a spirit.

Isn't love sacred? Isn't it something that you could never take back? This is a question to ask those still in the middle of turmoil. This is a thought to ponder because I perceive that once I realized <u>you are me</u> in the tempered waters, I could never hit extreme aversion. Yes is yes and no is no and with every disappointment, I have found it less difficult to fade from an undesirable situation, always knowing the truth about love and the consequences of its condition.

In a different couple's story, he was beautiful inside and out. In fantasy, I wanted him to put on his best suit and save me. He wore a tux with a top hat and as I thought about the possibilities of the night, my skin began to perspire. After my makeup was on, the ladies asked me to stand—but I was frozen in my chair. As they were fanning me, they came up with the only remedy that would allow me to walk. Imagine it: A lady, an alcoholic drink, an orange gown, an insolent-swagger and a pair of high heels—making their way into the arms of a Clark Kent with accepting eyes and beautiful dark skin. We danced and kissed past the slow songs of an evening prom and had to be reminded to separate our entwined bodies when the band pointedly changed its rhythm from slow to fast.

You are with me now and day after day, *you* became my admiration and showed up everywhere in the crowd. *You* gave me tips on games played in a man's world and listened to a girl drenched in impracticalities. Finally, true love was here. We were going to slip away like "babes in the woods" and fight for a moment to be alone. I lit some candles, turned the music to low and cooked his first meal to 1-800-the-man-is-mine.

Romance…and then one tear after another, I cried as I served him a burnt steak with charred potatoes and shriveled green beans. He offered a smile of kindness, ate with forgiveness and wiped away my embarrassment.

"You make me want to," so I fell into his arms and forgot about the vow of "I won't." "Lubb-dubb" and as my clothes started to fall away, an amazing line (made famous by my mother) sounded like a roar in my ears.

"A smile leads to a hug. A hug leads to a kiss.
A kiss leads to a feel. A feel leads to a lay.
And, a lay leads to a baby."

The room suddenly lost heat and as a different mood began to develop, my teeth chattered and... the room started to spin and... I fainted. Like a wilted lily with insufficient water to its stem, the girl suffered from a sudden reduction of oxygen in her red blood cells and she experienced intermittent syncopal episodes.

The flower was not ready to be removed from its root and the couple would endure and wait for the "ceremony." While adding salt, pepper, and other spices, they would make as many calls to each other as it took. They would write letters from a distance, meet goals to enhance their future and make decisions and mistakes that would eventually change their paths.

> Standing in front of the world and
> tasting—it is you! You are the memories
> that eventually allowed me to not be
> afraid of who I am and whatever I am.
> You are the one who will be with me in
> the water. You are my care and despair
> and the one who has sanctioned my
> knowing the truth about love and the
> consequences of its conditions.

———

A lot of people know the surface side of me,
The side they see while I'm working or just
Going through the day...

But there's another side of me
- An inside - that people never see.
It's a part that's full of a thousand thoughts;
A part that embraces love and cherishes friendship.
A part that understands without need for words.
A part that has yearnings and desires and prayers.
The inside of me has so many moods
That the outside never shows…
I feel like its ok to let someone in…
To let them see me
Emotionally and physically as naturally and
As naked as I can be.

Only You
By Jamie Delere

Chapter 10

WANTING TO

Remember that Saturday when **Wit** told me that I did not die? Now I stand here "Wanting to" and I should tell you what that means. Sure enough, it is an urge and desire to put someone like you or me on the front lines of finding ourselves more than once. Indeed, it is a stimulant that prompts us to make attempts to reveal our talents. It is a novel idea that gives us reason to stand right here, fall down and try again. In fact and fiction, "wanting to" thrusts a wish, propels a dream and eventually delivers something that is within us.

While on my knees,
the world is revolving around me
and so many thoughts
keep coming in and going out.

You see the baptism that I am to feel.

The water in the lake is ceremonial
and I can see right through it.
I am catching glimpses of myself,
and in this one moment,
I am telling you that I have written
what has led up to:

Me wanting to forge ahead in a dialogue,
which will allow me to eventually find the balance
and stand on solid ground.

I want to,
so
I tilt my head back
and do not expect to find myself
too high in privileged places.

I have exquisite taste and know that there is wine in this water. However, before I grandstand, I must tell you that discretion made me take a look at life's principle constituents.

What does this all mean?

It means that I am "wanting to" claim that I am no one and someone at the same time. It means that I can be down or up on my luck at any given interval. It means that I am mindless and senseless because they say I am. It means that I dare not put myself above or below the lyrics of being special. It says that I am romantic and conscientious. It indicates that I am pursuing the unknown and says that I am more than a single entity: ordinary, extraordinary, deep, philosophical, egotistical, idle, persistent, empathetic, foolish and still trying to figure out what I am supposed to do to live and survive in the fields inside and outside my mind.

You see the baptism that I am to feel:
As I fall freely,
Immersion in the tempered water tells me,
"Living is easy—but surviving is hard!"

You breathe in and out and the majority of the work is done for you; then you face the challenges that are beyond the imagination and the process of inhaling and exhaling suddenly becomes difficult.

As I hold my breath
and do not allow air to travel its course through my
pharynx, trachea, bronchi
and sophisticated lung segments,
it becomes evident to me that in a lifetime...
We are to figure out why, how, when and where.

Why me, you, we, us, them and they? How will I, when will I and where will I take steps to do something about my situation?

Still encapsulated and reflecting:

**This particular characterization
does not want to breathe another breath
without trying to fully work through
what is necessary to develop
graciousness, self-expression and truth.**

It is bizarre, but much of this heart-felt affair includes a simple configuration of menus, the right seasonings and the best presentations; which make us revel in their triumphant combination—when they are placed in front of us.

**Time under has now become a factor.
As I continue watching what is happening above me,
I see you approaching the banks of my situation.**

You must be speculating and telling yourself that this is all fiction but I can see you and you have not stopped yourself from wanting to put your hands in deeper.

Chapter 11 —

RISK

As I see you about to take a risk, I know that writing this down is leaving the doors of probability open for anything to occur. As I am putting myself out on my limbs, apprehension comes to mind and anxiety starts haunting my consciousness. "True fear" encroaches. And while you are reading my thoughts, ideas and recollections; it scares me that something could still turn me away—and I would never complete this.

EYES, I know that while many surround me, only a few can sense the phenomena happening within me. A couple of weeks ago, an acquaintance told me something that I was not up to hearing. They then reached out their hand and gave me a poem that I read everyday.

———

RISKS

To laugh is to risk appearing the fool.
To weep is to risk appearing sentimental.
To reach out to another is to risk involvement.

To express feelings is to risk exposing your true self.
To place ideas and dreams before a crowd
Is to risk their loss.

To love is to risk being loved in return.
To live is to risk dying.
To hope is to risk despair.
To try is to risk failure.

But risks must be taken because
The greatest hazard in life is to risk nothing.

The person who asks nothing;
Does nothing, has nothing, is nothing.

They may avoid suffering and sorrow,
But they cannot learn, feel, change, grow, love, or
live.
Changed by their attitudes, they are a slave.
For they have forfeited their freedom.

Only a person who risks is truly free.

RISK
Author "Betty"

This gift was befitting of this experience and is what I needed to follow through on putting "A TASTE OF ME" down and keeping it there. To be honest, I am hoping *risk* does not leave me daunted and unable to emerge into a better state of mind.

I am soaking wet and I am hoping you understand that this part of the story has nothing to do with them. Risk is individual and as I try to hold my breath for as long as I can, I know that it is only my choice to be free with all that flows through my hand. Yes, this is exposure and now that I have made up my mind to do this, it is up to you to do with it—as you wish.

So I rolled the dice and while under the water I saw myself writing a letter—to Eyes— on a soft roll of two-ply. It was my first attempt and I was hoping for a 7 or an 11 to land on the table. I told myself "either number" and just like that, the pen was in my hand and I was making plans to send the unedited, fragile, soft and cottony version to both of them.

I said to myself, **"Wit, Demon, Reticent, Creativity** and **Personality**; can you believe that we are writing on this paper? Are we full of it or am I reaching out to the comforts of those who are, versatile and absolutely detailed enough to understand more than the surface side of me?"

Eyes, you never hesitated to tell me who you were and you did not turn away when I pulled you aside after class and questioned your motives. Left and right: I watched

you share with a room full of strangers, contained my
thoughts and became transparent. I could hardly see your
face anymore. Hand after hand went up and as you took
on the judge and jury, all I could think about was: care,
dare, fear and despair.

Looking past all of this water and losing hope,
I sensed you wanted to save me.
But what good would that have done,
to let myself be rescued.

For once, I realized I needed to be my own hero
and I had to become visible.

So there I was in the third seat of the first aisle.
As you left the chair, I was scared for you. When you
headed to the front of the room, you were about to take
a risk and I would be safe—keeping the timer. Only five
minutes and just like that, each word of your sensitive
subject caught their attention, dared me to take part in
my own philosophy and resulted in everyone agreeing or
disagreeing in harmony. Wow!

How long do you think it will take for me?
How long do you think I can hold on?

I see your face, feel your hands and
get the sense that your gestures are urging me to
resurface to an initiatory right to celebrate.

**While I do feel myself coming closer,
many are watching and I am still:
questioning, speculating and wondering.**

Maybe I am wrong about people. Maybe I am wrong about them and they and us. Maybe someone does know a little bit about me and how I think and feel. One of my professors said: I stir the pot of our society with my poignant questions, with my unwillingness to settle for the generic answers that are supposed to solve life's riddles, with my probing the truth—until it makes it somewhat uncomfortable for those choosing to live lives of mediocrity.

Could she be right? Is this the part of me that will not settle and is unwilling to walk away from those many feelings, ideas and questions? Does someone else's view identify the depth of my risk or do they verify my suspicions; someone has made every effort to avoid the predicament of self and remain obscure?

Chapter 12

A CLUE

As time runs, walks and crawls, a moment tells me I have been in one state of mind most of my life. If I am to find solutions that will help me to become successful, I must find a way to pull the cobwebs off of myself. So take three steps forward with me and know that while I do have a clue on what's happening to me, I can not fathom what to do!

The arrows deep within me point in different directions and the unfamiliar part in all of this is being honest. Everyday the struggle continues; I keep writing and those small traces of evidence jump out at me and ask "What are you truly afraid of?" As the person telling this story, I feel so awkward and unable to answer—but once I lock into my Allies, there are signs that "I care." I care about you, your thoughts, your feelings and your welfare. The truth is, regardless of your decree, I am stirred and my heart is in the mix.

I am so nervous and the thought of you has me lost in my own truths and principles. For me you are the color of love. For them you are the warm wish that got away. Flow fast and then slow. Turn three-hundred-sixty-degrees and tell me how I got here. I duck under the radar and I fly as low as I can. I turn away from this sort of temptation and dare not to be a part of your world.

One half of my world consists of the fantasy of Zan. She has been and is a big part of my life. She is there for me through thick and thin. She listens to my silly thoughts and then puts up with my latitude and longitude. Zan and I are so close that we are at an angular distance of a celestial point, where we can never admit to the world how we feel. Hence, we distance ourselves from that deep place called intimacy. We go everywhere together until the world of reality interrupts our windmill. We then slow down our sails and post denial.

The last time I saw Zan, I wondered what year it was. It seemed like nothing had changed, until the highlight of the day made us both realize we were playing a futile game that we always insisted upon engaging in. The moment was profound but it warranted an "I love you and I always will." It left me questioning if the eccentric person inside of someone like Zan—wanted to tell me something.

So Eyes, this is all part of it. This is the part of being honest with you: me, he, she, they and them. This is the part of letting it all hang out and realizing that ignorance in this one life *is not bliss*. Bliss is abounding happiness that would have me stopping in my tracks, skipping into the absolute and wishing you would call so that I could tell you something.

I want to tell you that I understand so much more about life now and I appreciate your standing in time with me. I want to tell you that your voice still rocks me softly through hard times and your advice has me contemplating about the realities of a new year.

> In the here and now, I only wake up
> with thoughts of what I have to do
> today. I jump into the shower with
> the sound of the alarm still ringing in
> my ears. I start to feel the warm water
> welcoming me into the new day and
> finally: I open my eyes to the light
> and smell the scent from the soapsuds
> running off my body.

Cobwebs be free! Loosen your fine-spun network of art and help me share a tale. At five years old, Robert was a boy who acted like a girl. He never fit into the male classification of pure testosterone. He had a soft touch and a gentle character. He was auspicious to the eye but he could never be what a father thought a son should be.

At seven years old, I could type, paint, wire a house, build a black board and check the oil level under the hood of a car. I wore white and was trusting to the world. I sat with the eloquence of fine posture and one day, as I stamped in each printed character on my typewriter, Mr. Friend took away my innocence. I was never to be what a mother thought a daughter should be. Therefore, I put out to you the only true statement Red ever knew: "Boy and girl, white and black, and *different*!"

The world will always continue to rotate on its' axis, while we take on the experiences of fact and fiction— and create the products of life circumstances. As the inanimate became frigid, Red zipped herself up tight and occasionally tried to let someone know what made her different. She was dirty and confused. Every nightmare gave the second-grader a chance to fight back but her actions never changed the outcome. She was uninformed and always wanted to know if it were possible for Snow White to come back to life once again, to be pure and chaste and "As lovely as the bright day."

Breathe! As the child begged for someone to spare her life, Robert graduated from grade school and Red never saw him again. It has been reported that he died too young; he will never know that he was an innocent bystander helping an author to stand tall.

Eyes, if you could sense me, you would know that in fiction I have a clue but in fact I am so suicidal right now that my right brain feels my left hand blowing it away. I am off the page and looking for the words to say: "It is like killing the self and still living."

> I stand there on the ledge and *Thought* hopes you will call me prior to the last highlighter giving out—and just before the pencil that makes it all possible loses its lead. It is abhorrent but I am holding those undeniable feelings inside me and wondering why they haunt me in my dreams.
>
> *Thought* is lying in a dark night questioning life, ability, integrity, sanity and hope. So many IDEAS and OPINIONS; *Thought* is but an external surface walking with a stranger who stands alone at a crossroad. There are VIEWS at the center of my optical surface, but *Thought* is pointing me in multiple directions.

Yes! I, they, them, we, he, she, me and you may all have a clue; yet we still choose to get caught up in the scrutiny that confuses us and takes us away from our own qualities and sensibilities—which are meant to lead us to the truth.

Please excuse me for a moment, while I talk to myself.
I am asking you (those thoughts inside of me)

"Why?"

And I am telling you that it is time to let go.

Look at this! Have you figured out what I am doing?
I am getting myself together and sinking you into my story.

As I see it,
You tell me to live:
Yet, you say that I am stepping out of my place.
You tell me to speak, yet you tell me to shut up.
You tell me to let you know if someone is hurting me:
Then you are resistant when it comes to helping me.

In every account, as I come into my own likeness,
I write again and tell you:
"Stop dwelling in the darkest room in my mind."

I tell you to get a clue and as I find a solution <u>to me</u>,

I Say:

"You can stop taking me for granted."
"You can stop luring me away."
"You can stop being precarious."
"You can stop undermining me."
"You can stop encouraging me to quit."

"You can stop interfering with my best judgment."

Chapter 13

WISH AND DESIRE

It is only now:
I feel I am able to grab on to your hands
and step out of the water onto solid ground.

As I begin to breathe again and feel the subtle impacts of nature, I look at you and choose to live and be me. I choose to be satisfied with my choices. I choose to: smile and cry, be angry and happy, be honest without convincing someone it's truth, find positive in the negative, find play in the middle of a silent room, doubt only with cause, focus on the here, and prepare myself for now. It is a turning point and the time to take the ground dust and make this, describe this, and inscribe this. Wish and desire because:

There are no longer reasons to ask myself WHY ME and all the reasons to answer—WHY NOT ME.

Then I blink and realize that the sun is setting and the loving couple has distanced themselves away from the lake and beyond my view. How long have I been out here? I stand up and put my arms above my head. I yawn more than once and drag myself into the house. I reach for the on-button to the radio and dance all the way to the kitchen. I love the words of the song and I love how someone else's moment can take me back to reflect on my own particulars.

Such is this mood that has me putting myself in the room with fantasy. I start to dance and decide on "A TASTE OF ME." I am going to make Lemon Chicken and Risotto. I grab a saucepan and put in toasted rice along with bursts of water, chicken bouillon, butter and salt. It is on the fire and now I am into moving my head and putting a twist in my hips. I feel so good; and back and forth I go. After stirring the ingredients with a fork, I put the heat on low and cover the pot with a lid. Sure, it is not the best method but I have got to sing now and trust me—when I put Eyes in the room with me, I cannot keep up with their moves.

I pull a couple pieces of chicken out of the refrigerator and set them aside. I find the lemon, garlic, pepper and olive oil. As I baste, I wonder if anyone can hear me in the middle of making a new song. I call out and say:

"It is about that unsure feeling that tackles
you right in your tracks. It is about having a
sure thought every time you wake up—only to
disappoint yourself with a new thought the very
next day.   It is about a full plate and a blind date
that bubbles over and puts your heart on hold and
your head on spin."

"Eyes, it is my desire and my wish to be dancing
with you.   How sultry, as I watch the masculinity
in your tux and the femininity in your dress.
STEP, STEP towards me, and listen to me lift my
voice higher and higher in your song."

———

DESEO
(Wish and Desire)

*

When I put your eyes in my day
It seems that troubles are miles away
So let me start a slow sweet fight
While I'm traveling through the night

*

DESEO, DESEO
Let me risk my life

*

Hey, you inspire me, can't you see
You're dying to be free

Another day and I'll holler
Another way and you'll bother
To put your tears away
*

Hey, your eyes are guiding me
Your moves are making me
They're making me feel free
*

No woo-s
Put on your dancing shoes
Make your moves
*

DESEO, DESEO
Let me risk my life
*

Bring on desire
Bring on the fire
Bring on the burn
Make pieces of the heart yearn
*

Tiptoe
Let it all go…
DESEO
*

Let it all glow…
DESEO

We've got the flow…
DESEO

DESEO
For M.B.

The beat slows down and you seem to be pleased. Your hands wave in a frantic yes and your smile is illuminating. I stare at you and there is no telling what is going to happen next. I explore and imagine: If I put all of you in one dish, and serve you up as a meal, you would be full of zest and flavor and... Oh No!

It has been 20 minutes and the rice is done! I definitely got carried away and start to laugh at my struggle to sing this heart-felt song in key. Really, I do not sing well; it is best to just listen and hum to the melodies already playing. As I heat the required elements in the frying pan, I roll my shoulders and get the feeling—dinner is going to be good.

Bon Appetit!

Chapter 14 —

REMNANTS OF ANGER

As I savor the last meal of the day, I realize there is not much time left in this year. Provided with a moment to cast back, I wonder why so many people linger over the negatives. They use every opportunity to complain about their jobs, families, friends,—and what they don't have.

They become "Dwellers" who have a tendency to be taken over by unfavorable memories; and then change into something that you had no idea they could become. Negativity finishes first and in a scary movie its' victims consume anger and retaliate with mischief. Scene by scene, the plot thickens and negativity welcomes stress and eats them alive.

Day after day, we all wonder what happened to you. We hear what you say—but shut down to the repetition of your trials and tribulations. Is it remnants of anger or is it a wound interfering with the continuity of your character?

You stare at "stage-one" where there
is an insurmountable pressure on you
that impedes the human spirit. You
are reddened with a sad face and those
surrounding you must take notice. You
have tried to change your position but
the tissue is inflamed and you begin to
break down with a shallow "stage-two"
ulcer.

Who could understand what you are
going through? The ordeal is painful
and every time you turn to someone
for help, there is no support available.
Everyone is sloughing you off to
temporary solutions—for foul smelling
assaults. One door opens and another
one shuts. After more stress, anxiety
and frustration, you see a shining
moment of hope that somehow erupts
into a "stage-three" necrosis.

Not understanding you or your inability
to heal, they lock you in and give you
counseling that includes "debridement"
and "antibiotics." They cleanse the

wound, cover it up in dressings and
send you back into the same situation.
Everyone tells you that you look
remarkable. You smile a lot but no
one knows; something inside of you is
keeping you posted on an upcoming
"stage-four" nightmare.

Disillusioned, you continue to give
accounts of what you have been
through, but insist: The deep wound
does not hurt anymore and will not be
fatal. You "dehisce" more than once
and those in the background eventually
write you off as a chronic complainer
who is incapable of healing.

What happened to the empathy and the
sympathy for your woes?

———

It is a sad face in disguise and
A stern look with beautiful eyes.

You've got me wondering if you are blue,
You've got me wondering about the w-h-o in you.

Is something in there worth a smile?
Or is your heart forever on trial?

You know every now and then,
I and we can still see in.

SO SERIOUS ALL THE TIME

On and on! And I remember the beautiful woman I once knew. She was as sweet as candy and Sister said there was a time when she did not scream or curse. Her demeanor reflected what was in her heart and her ambitions kept her striving to make life good.

Well—it must have been a long time ago because that nice lady was eventually beaten down until she was forced to defend herself. In "fight or flight," she did what it took to be a survivor and learned how to use a word like a venomous blow. After many altercations with her husband: She endured, stood up, stiffened her chin and refused to be knocked out.

I gather I could spend a whole chapter on this and tell you how a woman's fight for survival and dignity changed my family's life. I could wind back down that road again and tell you how I started to believe those who treated others like crap had a better outcome. For whatever reasons, some folks are just cold and nothing can arouse them. They never seem to hurt and give those that are watching a false perception.

———

Maybe it is better to dish out affliction before receiving it. So I converted at my boiling point and began to dampen the warmth. When I reached zero-degrees, my surface was frozen solid. My form had changed and I found out about the damage that could be done—when the temperature was too cold.

Frost bitten by a bad experience, I became cold as ice and those around me began to pay the price. I was not sure what was left inside but there was pain under my pride. I gave the perception that I did not want the sun, for those around me could not have fun. Eventually I learned something from a friend, "It was time to forgive from within, if I were ever to feel the warmth again."

COLD AS ICE

I can tell you, that I think the sweet woman now carries remnants of anger like it is an addiction. Just when you think she is over the worst of a bad day, episodes from the past tack on to the problem; and there she is on the defense again. She can't hear the noise that she makes and you can't see her pain. I wish I could fix it! But I have no control over her remnants and can only work toward settling my own misfortunes.

I attempt to forgive and in my humbleness, I say I forgot. I set myself on the positive and look at all that Mother did right. Ultimately, she left me with the strength to survive, the motivation to press on and the attitude of importance. She gave me life and pushed me toward a better future with good intent. Most importantly, when it comes to the "Hierarchy of Needs," there was always a roof over my head and a meal in my day.

Mother worked days and nights. She found a way to afford her children a better education in a neighborhood that did not promote success. She taught us to be clean and it was imperative that her children knew: "Being poor did not mean you had to be dirty." She prayed while her offspring slept and gave you that special kiss and hug—exactly when you did not expect it. I would say "Yuck" which meant I could not stand taking that Cod-Liver oil; but I loved that she wanted the world for me.

In the midst of crimes surrounding my world, Mother was a promissory note ensuring that I saw events that made me happy and hopeful. I did see the worst but somehow I knew there had to be opportunities available to those who were committed to having them. I saw *optimism* in the Ice Capades, *enthusiasm* in the Globetrotters, *encouragement* in the 76ers and *feasibility* in The Wiz. I went to church whether I liked it or not. At school, I saw how the other half lived. Every Christmas there was something under a living tree. I was allowed to lick bowls during the holidays. I went to a camp in the Pocono Mountains—where I could actually look up and see stars that were not blinded by a polluted night.

It has been a hard lesson to learn but I now know that a remnant of anger makes you forget there were good days. It makes you unappreciative of what you had. It makes you unable to remember the essence of home cooking. It causes you to travel with pain, go without your smile, become bitter, stand still in the middle of growth, lose ground, spiral downhill and become something that will never heal.

Chapter 15—

DIGESTION

I digest as I sleep. For seven to eight hours, I sink into varying degrees of unconsciousness. As my body temperature falls and my respirations slow down, I allow relaxation to take over so that the vessel I reside in—can break down all that I have consumed and eliminate what is not pertinent to me. As difficult as this process may be, one must take steps to rid their body of negative influences.

It was like living in never-never land and you were my father. You were creator and ruler of my universe; the power, protector and provider of my life; and the best man chosen to lead me into the future. True or false! I loved you more than you could see; I believed in you more than

I believed in me. "That's my daddy," I would say. Then I needed to catch my breath!

———

Why would anyone say
you were at the center of a sad song
There was nothing my daddy could do wrong

I told friends you were out saving the world
Big Brother said
there was too much innocence in this daddy's-girl

He said you only gave your goodness to me
And that was something I did not see

Good or bad, you doted on your Red
And that brought your first born,
beating down on her head

He thought we had too much fun
But wondered why you never accepted him —
your first born son

Trying to understand, I held my daddy's hand
Trusting and believing he was the best man

They said you started bragging
about the good guy you were
As there were just a few that would concur

Suddenly thinking
your family wanted to get over on you
You hesitated to do for them, the best you could do

You carried a false personality
and plenty of chump change on you
Making other momma's easy to get to

Such disdain was felt when you complained
'Cause daddy's pockets were empty to his ball and chain

You did not have to take it that far
But you wanted to be a Movie Star

Exposing descendents of your paternity
To your rendition of ghetto atrocity

What happened to the fun
You drank, gambled and taunted your son

You always said what you were going to do
But you abused the love your family had for you

You killed their spirit and vitality
What did you think would happen to their mentality

I can't tell you about the depth of my pain
But I prayed all men were not the same

Mr. Wimp wore his tie and gloves
But he was not the man I thought he was

While toasting to the best of life
He stood as a coward, watching you kick your wife

Yes, he was your "bird of a feather"
That's why you guys flocked together

So as the glass crashed upon my mother's head
I knew the legacy of my father was dead

Lots of pain made the whole family insane
As we watched you run out, burned and in shame

What did you expect the woman to do
You beat her until she was black and blue

My fallen hero standing over six feet
Was a violent beast, leaving bad memories to keep

It was time for bed
And there it was, a gun full of lead

You put it straight to my head
I became a disillusioned Red

I guess it was supposed to be love
But what could a doting father be thinking of

Brother too scared to tell the truth
The police said they did not have enough proof

I never took a dime from you
Yet you accused me of stealing bonds; it was not true

You raped part of my mother's life
Leaving me behind to receive your knife

Under oath, you told the judge that I lied about you
But I was there watching everything you would do

Amazingly your children still wanted a dad in their life
While you spread rumors
and blamed all your troubles on your ex-wife

I truly could not fathom what my father had done
And a Grandma couldn't give up on her son

She told me if I did not want anything to do with you
It meant that she was out of my life too

Still thinking you were a king in your own right
You fathered other children in the night

You joined the church and claimed to be upright
Then confessed your sins in the light

Preaching and telling followers: "Be Free"
It is only your family that can truly see

Do not cheat, steal or condone
Yet the preacher can be overheard
cursing and gambling over the phone

I shattered when I heard the little girl say
Her daddy called her a "ho" just yesterday

Then you straighten up like the good guy next door
Getting back to the sermon on the floor

I got your genes and all sorts of bad things
That is the genocide you passed on: It stings

Yes you were my god, looking the other way
That's why I learned the act of plunder
while you were at play

So, as the preacher reads these words from long ago
He now understands how I digested
and found a way to let him go

Lots of therapy to rid regret
Forgiving all that I can't forget

So walking away from all the bother
I refused to dwell on a man I used to call my father

My Fallen Hero

While the good Lord took over for my father, I really needed to get away. "Please help me," I would ask: Then the Spirit let me know it was going to be alright. I traveled and found—the world was much more than my father's decay. Then tranquility set in and I realized the body cleansing process was very in depth, as some things took longer to let go of.

Good and bad, Mr. Brown was the daddy I was dealt. He was not the work of perfection but I will not be the judge of his infliction. He was not the worse that there could be and with faith who knows what others will be allowed to see.

Chapter 16 —

UNEXPECTED

Did you know that a helix is a spiral and in some dictionaries the word itself is followed by the word hell? Alright, that was inconsequential and the kind of thing that jumped into my mind *unexpectedly.* Whether it was funny or not, it does break up the monotony and cause you and others to heighten an eyebrow, twist a face and ask, "Where did that come from?"

I must be getting tired. I rolled from this bit of trivia into thinking about all those children. I remembered watching television in black and white and there they were: orphaned, sick, hungry and located in distant third world countries. Too young to understand, I asked many questions regarding the health and well-being of those unknowns. I did not get the answer I was looking for but was reminded there were hungry children in my own backyard.

I did not believe it at first, but then there was "Dirty Chuckey" and his unlucky brothers who lived right down the street. Dirty Chuckey was a nice boy but his teeth were black and rotting, his hair was always uncombed and his clothes were torn and dingy. Although Chuckey was addressed by his title, teased and made fun of all of the time—he never looked like the poor children on T.V. Despite rumors suggesting that he had no soap or food in his house: He did not smell bad, always smiled when he was around me and never complained or begged for a meal.

Although I never knew Chuckey's real name, he was my friend. Sometimes we sat on the steps, talked about the neighborhood, and fantasized about the kinds of things we were going to do when we grew up. Dad disapproved of this and made it clear that Chuckey was not the kind of boy that I would be spending time with. "Too bad," he had no idea that Chuckey had good career plans and was one of the smartest boys around. If he was hungry, it was for knowledge.

In school, the teacher reported, "There is enough food in the United States to feed every child." Mother said it was true, but considering where I lived and what I saw, I could not accept that statement. It seemed like every hungry kid showed up to eat at our house—and

I was tired of only seeing them at supper time. When it was time to eat, Dad would put his lips together and whistle. As his children started making their way home, the neighborhood crumb snatchers were not far behind.

You would think this type of behavior would stop after a divorce, and especially after the "clever one" cooked up a scheme and served a memorable snack: chocolate flavored dog vitamins coated with peanut butter and covered with morsels of bread. Delicious! It seemed very funny until *unexpectedly* some of the fools came back to the door, said they liked it, and asked my younger sisters for more. I could not laugh this time. My only intention was to ward the solicitors off and give them a good reason to eat at home.

There was an immediate change in my attitude and I was thankful for two things: I always remembered having something to eat and mom never found out about my practical joke. I was ashamed when I found out that my victims food sources were not what I thought they were. As I took a sudden interest in helping others: I stole from the rich, gave to the poor and made sure I cleared my conscience at the confessional. I stood in line at church and thought of ways to throw the Super-Power off. When it was my turn, I hyperventilated and told the man in black—big lies. Then, right in the middle of it, I would spout truth and wait for the holy man behind the screen to assign me at least ten "Hail Mary's" and a couple of "Our Father's." I would burst out of the door for air and find a place to play with my rosary beads. As my nose got shorter, I would lose track of how many prayers I had left. Then I would stare at the statues and ask them: "Why does that *box* smell funny and why do the old people kiss your dusty feet?" Waiting for answers, I hesitated but continued to give Mom's pennies to pan handlers.

When I was eligible for a summer job, I sponsored a food program that required I serve breakfast and lunch to the children in the neighborhood. Out of my garage, I served cheese, milk, juice, cereal, sandwiches, fruit, and cookies. The children were to pick up the meals and go home… but they hung around all day and my sisters and I became unpaid babysitters at an unlicensed daycare. I thought this first job was going to be easy— but *unexpectedly*, the children started coming over to get something to eat; "way-too-early" or "much-too-late." I think the most shocking thing was when I stepped out of my house to find two adults stealing food that I would have given to them.

Looking at the logistics: I had a hard time understanding this sort of behavior and spent days trying to determine if my neighbors were thieves or if they were just that hungry? Mom said to forget about the incident but I spent much time trying to make sense of their actions. Unable to ever look at those individuals the same, I contemplated the world I lived in and was already overwhelmed with reality. I could not imagine bringing a child into a world that seemed to be so cruel and ruthless. Therefore, like many before me, I vowed not to have children of my own—especially if I could not feed them, support them or move them to a better place. The grown-ups said that I did not understand, but I asked, "What was there to really understand, in a world that had plenty but excluded many?"

I was adamant about my promise because I grew up in a place that my European teachers and classmates insisted was the GHETTO. You have to capitalize the entire word, because it had special significance. According to the philosophers and politicians, it was a definite indicator in the human analysis and classification of my future. Certainly, most of today's young historians use the word as a symbol for coolness and popularity: but most have no idea of what it was to me, where it was, what it looked like and what could make it part of you.

Trust me, it was not just a neighborhood where those without would reside. *Unexpectedly*, it was a place where: Anyone who lived to talk about it, dared to forget it, promised to remember it and took a chance when revisiting it. If the walls could talk, they would say, "The GHETTO was a place where houses were packed so tightly together, that the sound in one home could be, heard in your walls." It was where you walked down the street and the trash lay around as if it had no other place to be. It was where a war began with bottles and sticks and ended with knives and guns. It was where a bullet had no name or age on it, but the food was good and the parties were what people now call "phat."

It is funny how you have no idea of what you are born into. Then one day, you just wake up to the whole of it. Who knows what was going on prior to your eyes really being opened? Maybe you had bits and pieces of a puzzle that made no sense. Maybe innocence was enough to keep you blind and then *unexpectedly:* I was the helix spiraling downhill, into a place that I thought was Hell.

Chapter 17 —

SLUM POLITICS

The slum was upside down and fear was in reverse of itself. You could not sit on your steps anymore and you had to put bars on your windows and lock your doors. Death was an honor for your son but not for his family. You watched talented NBA prospects play basketball, dunk drugs and sink into the cement of the schoolyard. You cooled down in the water plug, jumped rope, played Jacks with pieces of spiked metal and tried to dodge a ball to win. You enjoyed these times with your family and friends, knowing that in the script, they would one day: move, be six feet under or be learning how to shoot up and be glad—instead of sad.

In one spot on the map, I would *over-and under-exaggerate* to say, "Sometimes the place smelled like raw sewage." This was due more to individual erosion and corrosion than to refuse and debris. You could look at the architecture and its cohorts and find more beauty in a weed then in the wood paneling on your walls. Parents went to work and when revenue was not enough, they found shortcuts to feed their families— while their children found trades in the streets and became hoodlums molding into the actions of a well thought out novel.

The Politicians said that poor people simply abandoned their responsibilities. Debates took place and the "saviors" had many ignorant people believing: Things were going to get better if they voted. Viewpoints were in the wind and you would suddenly see people you never saw before. They would smile, shake your hand and get on the loud speaker and make promises. People were lifted up as if they believed the possibilities. Their sore eyes saw the winner get applause, while they were still trapped in their surroundings, received welfare, realized the color on their back and started to believe they would always be held back. The lady across the street would say, "Damn, they folded those promises up and put them in the brim of their hats!"

After each vote, my mother would say, "It doesn't have to be this way!" At the time she seemed to be the optimist, while the pragmatist looked around everyday to find something more clouding their way. People lived on top of one another and when they attempted to branch out, they found themselves nudging and taking things that did not belong to them. It was a true study of "cause and effect," as young boys were already baited for entrapment, while their outspoken art crimes defaced America—in attempts to get someone's attention.

I wanted to be more comfortable there. I wanted to believe it when I was told, "The world is a much bigger place, where the possibility of success is at least equal to that of failure." I wanted those pep talks about being proud of who you are and where you come from to be stimulating, but they did not excite me. I wanted the politicians to keep their promises and parents to practice more of what they preached.

I believed the parents and children who lived in the slums were tired of being humiliated. At any cost, they hoped for something better but were driven to become: the best hustlers, dedicated drug dealers, crafty thieves and deadly gangsters. This did not happen to me; but every moment I spent there, I thought I would grow up to become one of those individuals who had no potential—but all the ability to repeat what was handed down to me.

I heard that things could have been worse. I could have found myself in a place called the "Projects." It was the part of the ghetto where you looked up and saw layers of publicly funded housing developments falling out of the sky. Three-K said scarier stories came out of those places—and after seeing it myself, it made sense to me why so many juveniles were more than willing to spend time in jail. In a nut-shell, you got more "Buck-for-the-Bang" and for once, you had a taste of what someone else had.

Jail was no deterrent. It was like eating Louisiana hot sauce after swallowing the Habanero pepper. Back in the day, jail was like a well known dealership where you could "work while you wait." It was structured, heated and may have smelled better. Although parents and teachers said it was nothing to be proud of, it offered healthcare, religion, trades, gym privileges, visitation and access to books and education. If that did not interest one's mentality, maybe knowing most of their friends were there—helped in their decision making. Sure, there was violence, rape, and disease but why should that matter? "Everyone already told you what you would amount to…and you thought you were going to die anyway." The idea of a better life or a longer life had no meaning!

I recall trying to register for some high school classes. I wanted to take Chemistry because it was something I needed for the medical field. When the advisor saw my list of courses and found out that I wanted to be a Doctor or a Nurse, she just laughed and told me how preposterous my plans were. I could barely hold my head up, but the woman made me take a look at my grades and then told me, "That is just a pipedream!" She then signed me up for typing, stenography and home economics.

Who was fooling who about jail? I was nowhere near the top of my class and I understood at the earliest age that jail was not a Turkish Prison. For many it was just home away from home and an industry designed to make revenue off of the backs of ignorant people. A rat in the cell was nothing but a field mouse compared to your neighborhood sewer-cats; and a hardened criminal was often safer behind bars than he or she was driving through their own neighborhood. Who needed to research this? This was not an urban myth. It was real life, my very own interpretation and my imagination getting the best of me.

With all that going on, I eventually became paralyzed with a phobia that made me and my Allies more comfortable staying within the confines of my house and my mind. **Reticent** would search for reasons to be a hermit and the very thought of doors opening brought moments of sweat and anguish. "Please don't make me go out!" And my family never understood: The characters inside of me were doing everything to keep me alive.

Sure! I was fed lots of rubbish. Things were going to get better! "Those worse off would still be standing because they knew the struggle and how to survive it." **Wit** knew the strategy behind the word "Empowerment" but **Demon** knew the ghetto had already taken its toll on me.

As extenuating circumstances dominated all the riddled statements of hope, I was in "angst." To me, it was not a joke to be locked out in the open air; so I knocked, bawled and begged until someone recognized I was in marked distress. I remember going to see a child psychologist but I knew I did not have an irrational fear. As soon as I was old enough, I had plans to get away—so I guess I did things to R-U-N my therapist off.

As I stand inside of today, telling you about yesterday, "Slum Politics" made me realize the optimist was in just as much fear as the pragmatist. For instance, Mother did not speak matter-of-factly. She screamed at you and constantly repeated her no-nonsense lesson plan:

1. Educate yourself so you can educate your children!
2. Get married before the baby!
3. Have all of your children by one man!
4. Make sure the man loves you!
5. Save your money for the unexpected!

How ironic. My young mind was drenched in the GHETTO where marriage was a joke that never lasted. Dad vowed love, beat his wife and cheated openly. The majority of kids had the same mother but different fathers. The boys would not make it to be grown men and my older brother was fighting everyday to prove himself a man. Old guys found pleasure in little girls and some women would be found in trash cans or in places that left them unrecognizable to their own parents. A gangster blew a hole in a young man's head while my youngest brother sat on the dead mans lap. A man killed his nagging wife in front of his children and in front of me.

What was I to do with all of this history and when was the rest of the world going to recognize the third-world that was sitting in their backyards? How was I and so many others like me going to fully recover from so many incidents of violence and manipulation? Who was left to trust? Who would really fix the problems? How were people going to get out and who was going to stand up and truly represent them? It is a paragraph of familiar questions, and to date, the politicians continue to debate the issue and fix them with band-aid solutions.

As the echoes of frantic voices begged their children to listen, my mother's noise got caught in my middle ear. I would shake my head from side to side, slap one side of my face, and shudder. I was not deaf, dumb or blind and surely my siblings and I were smart enough to realize we were born in Hell. We saw people burn up from the inside out. When drugs took over, every man was for himself and there would be no coalition. It was like unsolved mysteries—and in Area 51, on the south side, people were test animals placed in a maze of confusion. It was another secret and regardless of the colors in a rainbow, folks were deemed "lowest class" and in a predicament that left them unable to understand the significance of my mother's strict sessions of instruction.

With one ear open and the other one closed, I turned my back on hope. I was certain the windows in the world would not open opportunities to me. By now, the unexpected had surely become expected and I was caught in a jam and conspired to think it was like that everywhere. No way would I consider other possibilities. No way could I take on wishful thinking. No way could I deal with more than one day of *thought* at a time.

As I tried to figure out what I was going to do, I remembered that Mother had a lesson plan. For what it was worth, I was fed up with slum politics and was going to stick to her proposal; that is, until I could find and execute my own.

Chapter 18 —

CHARM

I was thousands of miles away, and Charm was a beautiful boy who raised my awareness that parenting was both a risk and responsibility. It is easy and hard, a joy and pain, a reliance on old and new, a question and answer, right and wrong, give and take, innocence and guilt, present and future, patience and understanding, success and failure, family and friends.

The infant was not mine biologically but he was blood that smiled, laughed, suffered with ear infections and had temper tantrums every time we drove past a McDonalds. Despite daily efforts to show him pictures of his mother, he called me mommy and scared every male prospect away by calling them daddy.

After days and nights of struggling mentally and financially, I wanted to know how I could be having trouble caring for the well being of one child—when my parents had to rear six. I read some parenting books, gave individual attention, learned how to talk like Kermit (the frog) and ran myself ragged. This was hard work: and after food, pampers, utilities, daycare, a car note, and medical co-payments—I was tired and broke.

The boy occasionally refused his vegetables. When I dressed those plants up and convinced him to eat a little, he would upchuck and leave me cleaning a nauseating mess. Innocent and guilty; and, how many times do you think the daycare called me at work to say, "Your child is sick." I would notify my supervisor and run out the door with my work still in my hands. I could not fathom what it could be this time but the boy was burning up! We sat in the waiting room and as usual, someone was waking us to be seen. The Doctor told me it was another ear infection—and to answer the same question that I always asked; the person would look at me and reiterate that it was normal for a child to bring home illnesses that other children acquired. I was sure this was the explanation given to every parent and insisted I had done something wrong.

Turns out, I was on a first name basis with the Pediatrician. I called him many times and became one of those over-protective parents who panicked every time she thought about something happening to her sister's child. Charm and I became joined at the hip. I did not venture far without him and the secret space under my desk became a refuge for him in future days of sickness. Yes, I had done the unthinkable but it was the only way not to miss work, and a single parent solution to keep a boss happy and content.

During my period of adjustment, family and friends chipped in to take away holiday pressures. They brought gifts—while I became a discount barber and an occasional sitter. I clipped coupons and found that Depends were much cheaper than Pampers. What a deal! And then I opened the big bag and called myself a dummy: Those things were for adults and not some sort of generic diaper.

"Waste not Want not" and after days of Charm running around, heavily taped in his Depends—and after nights of him falling asleep to my heartbeat; I was happy that we were far away from my birthplace and even considered the day I would have a child of my own. Although once prudent, I was changed. I saw much more of the world and surmised that every stage was not the same. I started to believe, goodness could conquer the past!

Once I realized I could finally handle something, I was not ready when my sister returned from her overseas tour to take her child away. It was not supposed to be anything difficult. We worked out all of the details prior to her leaving and the day of return was sure to come. I was not to show my emotions but just as things started to make sense and I was coping, I became dispirited.

———

You are sitting on the bench
and watching the crowd pass
Never knowing a stranger would become
someone special in your path

Oh little joy, when you stumbled in my way
I did not see you as the miracle in clay

A look in your direction
leads to some sort of connection
Then hello and goodbye says affection

Off goes curiosity and wonder
As you bounced through the revolving door
like thunder

I took the time and learned where you had been
And together we shared what lies within

Hey special child in the roadway
Did you hear what I had to say

You are someone special who crossed my path
And it takes more than a calculator
to add the love that I have

Like that odorless, tasteless mixture
My love will be a fixture

Oh how I wish that you could stay
But as I watch you get further and further away

My adoration for you shall always stay
To carry on through what had become
an endless day

SOMEONE SPECIAL JUST CROSSED MY PATH

When Charm left, I understood that it was not easy
raising a child and there was no way I could have been
a perfect parent. I realized that you, me, us, them and
they are the children who grow up to meet the world
and everything in it. We all need guidance, TLC and a
certain amount of time to get our hands dirty—and a lot
more time to keep them clean.

After parenting, I appreciated my mother even more.
I was thankful I knew my father, and was grateful to my
older sister. When I thought about all the people who
discounted my efforts and told me "There is nothing like
having your own child," I wondered if they had ever
experienced anything like this. Did they really know
what they were saying or did they simply hear a woman
telling a child, "I want to be your mommy?"

I thought about Charm all of the time. He was his
mother's incantation and my appreciation. He was a life
my sister wanted and refused to end, despite anyone's
disapproval. He was kin but I told myself I could not

ever do it again. Emotions ran very high and then too low; I never knew if the child would come and when he would go.

It took some time to readjust. Then, at twelve years old, the baby boy who walked away—flew back into my life. Upon arrival, it appeared that he had formed his own set of internal characters. They were larger than life—and a part of this young boy who had been viewing the world through a small window in the ghetto. There was no way I could have been prepared for the troubles that we were about to face.

Chapter 19

EMBRACE ME

At age twelve, Charm was a happy and sad face. He was a dweller with articulate aggression and violent anger...a confused, well-mannered juvenile delinquent; a lost soul and a bright and crafty boy who wrote poetry and became resistant to himself.

I hardly knew who he was and when the store owner asked him if I was his mother, he erupted and put the guy in his place. What was going on and how did we both wind up in that vulnerable position again? Not too long ago, he was a boy holding my hand and now he was someone I did not recognize.

———

The Woman: *I want to be your mommy*
               The baby stood up

and reached for my hand
He bonded with joy
But did not understand

It is time to go for a ride
Even though this is something
we both have not tried
So give a tight hold
As your life will start to unfold

Tick-Tock as the boy
slowly grows into a man
Tick-Tock as he begins
to explore the land

The Child:

You hear my heart
But you can only play the part
'Cause you aren't my mommy
So do not pretend and stand by me

You can't love
Not with that iron glove
So at any cost
I pray for you to get lost

No way, you can't understand
Not like a real mommy can

You are my "dis"
And my remiss
'Cause I want to do nothing and
You always want something

You go against my grain
Then you too shall feel my pain
I am hurting, you fronting fool
Don't you know
only a blood mommy can be cool

I will spit in your face
If you do not give me my space
And know I will choke you down
Until my real mommy is found

I told you to die
But you continue to spy
And now I have to kill you
As I watch your blood spill too

Are you in fear
of what you will discover
Or do you still care,
as would my mother

The Woman: *With my last breath,*
I said to the troubled young man
I am still with you
and doing what I can
So won't you still try me
I am the mommy,
standing right by thee

I WANT TO BE YOUR MOMMY

I was sure the young man and I needed help. He told the counselor he was going to be with me until he was eighteen. I knew he had no idea of what that meant and was satisfied with me being his guardian—as long as I was his best friend, and not the parent that I turned out to be.

Charm began to have others call him Michael and he changed before me every day. I think I was supposed to learn something from this and as I watched his awkward character, I realized everyone of us is here on our own behalf. In one sentence, our parent's agenda is not necessarily the agenda we chose. We need individual attention and a key that may unlock our dreams and not the desires that our parents had for us.

Never say you won't ever taste it again! Never say what you can't do or won't do for those you love. I was concerned and exasperated. Charm's activities and schoolwork seemed to be a burden on him and a gift could never just be a gift. I encouraged friends but it turns out that paper and pencils were the only things that mattered and the boy's emotions were straight up and then straight down. He had mentors, but they were never as important to him as his absentee father: The man called intermittently, got the boy's hopes up and disappeared. It was maddening but as the donor-dad dropped off all together, rap and the power of God became his son's only goals.

When I went to a new job orientation, the woman spoke and said that she did not apologize for the hospital being a faith-based institution. She spoke about God and pointed out that he sees us as precious, valuable and of worth. She asked me to see what I did as more than a job. The woman prayed for me, you, us, them and they; and she asked that we always have compassion, respect and care.

> What a message to get, when I just told
> myself that there is nothing else that
> I can do for you. I think about you
> nonstop and in one morning, I knew
> that through your painful journey I
> could still be there to let you know that
> you are loved and that you are of worth.

> I am listening to you but I will not lower
> my standards—because that would do
> you a disservice and it would mean I am
> not committed to you. Believe it or not,
> I am more than an aunt. I am a parent
> that loves her child and will die loving
> him. You have innate dignity and you
> have it because you are here.

> No sir, I am not asking too much of
> you and I do not apologize for placing
> special emphasis on the values that
> I share with you. You call me "You
> people" and you tell me I am the source

of your pain. If that means that I
believe you belong here, and if it means
I refuse not to give up on you, then I am
guilty.

If it means that I will continue to
love you, even after you purposefully
sabotage yourself and refuse to accept
your ambassadorship to life, then I am
guilty again and most certainly ready
to face my crimes on what you called
Judgment Day.

It seemed like everyone else knew what was best for someone in my situation. Everyone knew exactly what they would do and after therapy and countless attempts of trying to do things a different way, I could only hope that a hug at the end of the day would help lift some of the boy's pain.

———

EMBRACE ME

It is too hard here,
which appears to be everywhere!
He cries, he screams.
He whispers to me, I want to be free.
Free to imagine what is not real.
Free to express exactly what I feel.
Life is not supposed to be a thorn in my side,
He calls out, where is my God?

Have you tried I asked the lonely child?
He shrieks and shakes as nothing applied.
Please do not push me away,
Know your God is here everyday.

Embrace me and accept what is true,
Thus life is a test God must put you through.

Your wants and needs will not be met,
Not until your heart has cleared
the ominous threat.
Pay attention to every subject and
Be sure to listen without reject.
Open your eyes and learn to cry and
Open your heart and promise to try.

Fly in your mind and dream in your soul,
Then look at your God to console.

Embrace me now, embrace me then
And when you're upset read this again.

EMBRACE ME
For Charm

Chapter 20

BEHIND THE BARS
OF YOUR MIND

The nights were getting longer and when stress hit me head on, I would cook. It was not something that I was good at but it calmed me. I fried and cried—until I figured out the dilemma that had nothing but everything to do with me.

As I saw a boy becoming a man, he fought growing up and asked me to preserve the child in him. I saw many talents in his book of rhymes but started getting worried that he would lose sight of things. Then, like a drama with twists of horror: My nephew acted on his impulses and spun out of control with delusions of his persecution. Distressed, I had to call to tell his mother that he was behind bars. I could hear the "What" on the other end of the phone as I tried to explain something that I did not understand myself.

For me, it was like watching a movie in a dark theater. Our talented son stepped into the room from behind the glass. I picked up the black phone and listened to him say someone was staring at him. He jumped from one thought to the next; and suddenly wanted to tell me a story about a made up "G-odd" who he claimed was infinite.

> In his scenario, G-odd was bored in his state of perfection. So in the odd god's dream, he invented people like you and me to bring about fun, action and adventure. Charm said, "We were G-odd's entertainment: We had to keep him laughing, intrigued and in suspense so he did not have to wake up to what always was (reality). When I asked what would happen if this G-odd woke up? He said "We would not exist."

> In Charm's story, the human species was called the Arynx. They had mystical powers, believed in having fun 24/7 and existed because G-odd was still laughing. Charm said, "Thus far the odd god's dream and the Arynx have been everlasting. In fact, G-odd never interfered with anything they chose to do and they now have

ancestors: Something no one could have predicted."

The story was good but concerning.
Before I could tell him how I felt about
it, the guard interrupted—it was time
for me to say goodbye. I hung up
the phone and I gave him a sign that
I would be back to see him again. I
turned towards the door and hoped that
one day Charm would write his story
down so we could revisit and discuss the
world he found.

Then the Detention Center door unlocked and I
walked out of the room. I could not help but think the
story explained Charm's attempt to escape from his own
reality. On my way home, I stopped to pick up the mail
and there it was—a letter from my nephew. It was one of
his rhymes, written for me. As I began to read, it said:

———

FIRE IN THE SKY

There's a fire in the sky
Can you see it
I can
I see the fire that burns in the hearts of men
The spark of attraction
and its potential of love for a woman

A wife, a daughter, a mother
The feminine offspring of the masculine
Three women I respect more than the almighty
The one I speak of is an aunt named Heavenly
A second mother to me
An understatement it would be
to call her a thing of beauty
The proper compliment is not in my vocabulary
She raised me from a hill with two or three small trees
To a mountain taller than Everest with loving necessity
She gave me knowledge
that I never asked for nor wanted
My know-it-all attitude was my shield so I fronted
I was pitiful when I cried
I'm sure I looked cute when I lied
But "Mommy" still rewarded me with a warm behind
When I had the nerve to defy
what was proper and right
Every welt on my booty
brought me even closer to the light
Good times came a plenty
Bad times too
So many memories I have
Let's keep-em straight and true
Reese's penis accidentally ordered at the dairy queen
We both busted up at the scene
Graduation from eighth grade
Food off the hook at Ms. Jewels; where I first got paid
Physical fitness in the gym, pools in which to swim
First CDs, discussion after discussion, Pockets and Mali
Fish incident, toilet water overflow
Appropriate terms for the words gangsta and ho

All of those and many more
in which we laughed and cried
Still, my question is why
You treated me better than Christ
When I die you'll inherit the essence of my life
One of the few kindnesses I was given by God
was an aunt
She did not run avaunt
She took my scarred mystique
And made it into something unique
A responsibility that wasn't even yours
My dark side taunts you endured

FIRE IN THE SKY
By S.J.R.B

I reread what was written and that's all it took to let me know; Charm understood the challenges we were going through; heard things I was trying to teach him; but most importantly, he knew that I would be there for him no matter what. I could finally lay my head down and get some rest. It was the longest day of the year: And I would wake up to find myself standing on more solid ground.

So embrace me and go back to the lake and put it all together. You should realize that reflections in the water just might be another story about you and me. It might be giving your own life another try and realizing you might not be the only one who needs to take the next step.

Life is a shared story and once you get an idea of who you are—a "TASTE OF ME" is food in the middle of your life. It feeds you, educates you and then empowers your individual flavors to become prominent, prideful and positive. "Lubb-dubb," I was writing freely. Then, I received an alarming phone call—and had to drive cross country.

There were no longer reasons
to ask WHY ME
And all the reasons to
answer WHY NOT ME

Eyes closed so tight that
they are wide open
I bow my head and fall to
my knees

While on my knees
the world is revolving
around me and
so many thoughts keep
coming in and going out

You see the baptism
that I am to feel

The water in the lake is
ceremonial and
I can see right through it

I am catching glimpses of
myself
and in this one moment

I am telling you
that I have written
what has led up to

Me wanting to forge-ahead
in a dialogue

Which will allow me to
eventually find the balance
and stand on solid ground.

I want to
So I tilt my head back
And do not expect
To find myself high in
privileged places

What does this all mean

You see the baptism
that I am to feel

As I fall freely
Immersion in the tempered
water tells me
"Living is easy
but surviving is hard"

As I hold my breath
and do not allow air to
travel its course through my
pharynx, trachea, bronchi
and sophisticated lung
segments

It becomes evident to me
that in a lifetime
we are to figure out

Why, How, When
and Where

Still encapsulated and
reflecting
this particular
characterization
Does not want to breathe
another breath

Without trying to fully
work through what is
necessary to develop
Graciousness, self-expression
and truth

Time under has now
become a factor!

As I continue watching
What is happening
above me
I see you approaching
The banks of my situation.

Looking past all of
this water
And loosing hope

I sensed you wanted
to save me

But what good would
that have done,
To let myself be
rescued.

For once, I realized
I needed to be my
own hero
And I had to become
visible

How long do you think it
will take for me?
How long do you think I
can hold on?

I see your face,
Feel your hands
And get the sense that
Your gestures are urging me
To resurface to
An initiatory right to
celebrate

While I do feel myself
coming closer
Many are watching and I
am still
Questioning, Speculating
and Wondering

You can stop interfering
With my best judgment!

It is only now
I feel that I am able to grab
on to your hands
and step out of the water
and onto solid ground

There are no longer reasons
to ask myself WHY ME
And all of the reasons to
answer
WHY NOT ME

Reflections In The Water

Chapter 21

WRITING THE DREAM

Dear friends, as I am rushing back to the place that almost consumed me, I am on another part of this journey. At a loss for words, how I wish I could capture my thoughts in poetry. However, it's just best to say Two-V is having a life threatening emergency and there is a long stretch of road before me. I really do not mind the drive and place my pen in my hand; steering it in the direction of life's poetry.

As you have seen, it is easy for me to cut ahead of or behind a paragraph or two and then place a verse before I get to the next stop light. I am not exactly sure how this form of expression came to me but the measured words and language find a way to complete my sentences. As a child, it transported my emotions and was a powerful interpretation of feelings that were misunderstood by most people.

Poetry was a key element throughout my life. Although I do not know much about the rules, poetry put itself on my road map and stirred something within me. Then it helped to heal my wounds and challenged me to create harmony in the midst of dreadful conditions. I tried to get a little elaborate with it, but my Allies advised me to keep the words simple, yet hidden from the naked eye. It was similar to my not so pretty face that I covered with hats—much like Celie did in The Color Purple.

As I fill up my tank every four hundred miles I can say that I was brave in the verses of poetry, but in my life I was afraid. Let's see, how can I put it? Ok, I have it. I was genuinely scared of people; I locked down my own mind and burned down all the unclothed words that were not written as poetry. I think I actually got to the point where poetry was the only survivor left in me to express my feelings. It was an avenue to drop off the hurt and a street to leave my pain.

It is amazing how far I have come in my own understanding. I finally reach my destination, park my car and go in to see what is going on with Two-V. As I continue to write, my dream is vivid and everything before me provides a brand new way of looking at my life. How can I take anything for granted and how can I help someone who can hardly help them self? I sit at my sibling's bedside in a daze. As I try to take everything in, it is starting to get late, I am exhausted and visiting hours are over. I am asked more than once if I am ok. I nod my head and whisper "I am."

I needed some time to think and suddenly understood why it is easy to give up on finishing a literary piece. Things make sense to the writer but not always to those willing to test a sample of their work. Changes are made for clarification but there is a tendency to lose flavor. There is a detour in the route and consequently, it may take time to get back to the true meaning of what is written. There is always something else that needs to be done and who knows what will happen in an emergent situation. Thus, distraction provides interference and when you take days off to rest your ink-filled utensils you suddenly lose intensity and slow down. For comparison, just as muscles atrophy due to less function, "will" can become a perpetual wish that never fulfills itself.

As I lay down my heart, I can tell you that it has been a trying year. Every time I say, "I will," the walls fall down around me and say, "You won't." Rushing out to fix a small leak leads to a large hole that needs more than a patch. When that job is done, my throat hurts and it takes more than Vitamin C to cure me. In the middle of taking antibiotics, I find out that my child has to clean out his locker. Just when the principal and I develop a solution, I hear that a family member is fighting for her life following a cerebral accident.

I was coming to—when a team of medical students were circulating in my sister's hospital room. The doctor explained, "It was a sudden rupture of a blood vessel" that found its way in Two-V's head. I immediately thought, "The third leading cause of death and the leading cause of disability are trying to implant and cause extensive damage to the likes of me." I am petrified thinking about the after effects and find myself weary and justifying why Two-V had to be included in the statistics of this embolus. So as I find some time to cry, I take nothing for granted and become increasingly aware that no one is without a problem.

Days become nights and I am trying to get through this occasion without a poetic explanation. As I watch my sister's head heal, I believe that dreams can come true. However, we can not and must not give up before they are actualized. Every day is a new beginning and a better chance at what you did not get right the day before. Every day is feeling quivers in your heart and feeling thunder rock the world below you. Every day involves trying it a different way.

So I stood up and urged my sister to respond to me. I talked to her and told her "I have a dream." Now you might say that those familiar words are part of a speech: A well documented oration of words that expressed thought while making a request for Civil Rights. History will tell you, it was put forth on the steps of the Lincoln Memorial to let people know—there was an injustice of freedom and equality when it comes to "all men" being treated as equals.

Words standing tall and breaking down the realities of freedom landed in Washington D.C. They screamed out to inform all audiences; there was an outright violation of the Emancipation Proclamation. High and low, words were defined in Dr. Martin Luther King's speech, which will be debated and reinterpreted over and over again.

As you read the excerpts, there is constant repetition of: "I have a dream today" and "let freedom ring." Getting a little further, you may realize the speech was given with the imagery of a man's dream to inform us hopefuls of the possibilities mounted in the dawn of a new day. So I ask, "When shall the words provide direction for you and for me?" I hope it is "starting today!"

I was not sure if Two-V could hear anything that I was saying. I then told her "I am writing the dream." It is surviving a crisis, abolishing all that is synonymous with a loss and surrounding it with a win. It is an adventure in fine dining where today's special is a delicate word surrounded by the sweetness of spirit, the narration of metaphors and the security of my own literary style. It is creating and appreciating that no one has it all figured out. The nurse walked into the room. She could see I was not going anywhere that night and brought me a recliner chair. After trying to reach Two-V, I sat down and looked around the room to make sure the environment was secure. Before long I was dozing off and felt compelled to have you look back in the mirror with me. I tell you to say:

> *"I love you,*
> *I love myself, I am beautiful,*
> *I am strong, I am capable and I will not give up."*

It is you talking to yourself and me talking to you. I want you to develop your mantra and destine it to be more than a wish. I ask you to:

Turn down the lights and brighten up your life. Stand in your world and on your rooftop. Meet the sunsets that pretend to not be in your reach. When night and day become one, put all of your worries away. Sew your weakness into strength. Ride high on the Ultra-light over a building in the sky. Tell the world you passed over the sea, and the land below felt your energy. Shout out what you feel and "let freedom ring." Do not be concerned about what you did not learn in May and concentrate on the lessons to be learned this day. Then, in a devout petition, write the dream.

Listen to you and listen to those declarations, "starting today!" Empower your testament. Do not fear the possibilities in your own existence. Stick with reality in your state of FICTION and recognize FACT will be the most significant amp of voltage in a world of mystery, magic, and manifestations.

I HAVE DREAMS and SO DO YOU!

Chapter 22 —

HAPPY NEW YEAR

Everyone is entitled to his or her own philosophy. It results in logic that allows you to sit down with a half-cup of fact and a pound of fiction. It is determination in your own message and belief in a pair of beautiful hands laying themselves upon Two-V and me, giving us newfound strength in tumultuous conditions.

You know it is one of the most celebrated holidays—and just before midnight, I decide to no longer let someone else determine who I am. I design my own road map, submit to the generosity of spirit and speak for myself! I make the resolution and it is another beautiful promise made in the advent of a new year. You are right there enjoying the moment with me but thinking "It is a self-solicitation, where one makes a dare and fills their mind, body and soul with good cheer." In this state of contentment, I am smiling yet wondering what my words and spirit will be like tomorrow.

Two-V is making a comeback. She is looking straight ahead but she is starting to blink occasionally, move her mouth and lift her hands. Everyday, mother and I massage the girl with oils—and the nurse tells us that we are doing a great thing. He says it is "Holistic Energy Therapy." When he walks away, I tell Mother that he is talking about healing a person through touch. It is something that many of the people I work with believe in.

> It is the count down and I whispered to a child,
> daughter, sister, mother, parent and friend—"You
> can do this!" The ball drops in Time Square
> and everyone raises their glasses and says
> "Happy New Year." Too bad I did not have a
> real drink. I watched the T.V., stood up for the
> commencement, drank my soda and made a claim
> that my life, Two-V's life, our life and your life
> won't ever be the same! I beat the metal side rails,
> turned up the music and acted like the people
> on the streets of New York were celebrating with
> Two-V and me. There was a party going on and
> in a budding thought, us girls were not going to
> miss it. I knew the nurse's aide was coming to tell
> me to keep it down but I just needed that brief
> moment to smile and laugh out loud.

SMILING and LAUGHING
(Risueña)

It is my perception to stop by
and have your forewings stand still,
So that I may whisper words that bring harmony
Into your semicircular canals.

Risueña!
As I am loving and living
and breathing in the waterway,
Then running and believing in this first day.

Do you feel the shift in your inner ear,
As you are moving into the New Year?

Can you feel the vibrations
transmitted in the atmosphere?
As your oaths resonate
while you are standing right here.

Find your balance when up and down.
Know you are navigating your life all around.

Risueña!
Listen to the internal me.
It is time to be worry free.

Quivering in a single pulsation
and putting your ear towards the sea,"
Hearing the words
"Blessed, Beautiful, Strong and Capable" Yes, it is me!

RISUEÑA

Happy New Year! I name this contingent period, "The Prelude of You and Me." It is an introduction that is free in its preliminary form. It is a composition that resembles an improvisation of change. It is all of me calling out to all of you to do something you have always wanted to do.

By the time the nurse's aide arrived, the party atmosphere had changed; he was looking around and wondering if he had the wrong room. The music was off, my legs were crossed and I was writing and devoting time to many word inhabitants. I thought about how my family was coming together during a crisis. My older sister talks to Two-V, repositions her body and settles the girl in. Dad prays over his child, while the rest of the family does the best they can. Friends can't be forgotten. They come in for a visit and wonder if our efforts and hope—is our protection from pain and suffering.

I am full of cheer and happy for this moment, I am appreciative of all I have and thankful for my life. My desire is for the year to be special for every one of us. I want it to be unique and I want it to be ours! I stand and say, "Look, listen and feel; then open your arms and reach out for all that you need." Sharing some recognizable and unrecognizable conditions, I am getting hungry and would like to go to a mystical place where atypical characters gather to chitchat and satisfy their appetites. My stomach grumbles and I have already developed a plan for myself and for Two-V. It is a good feeling but maybe I should not get too far ahead of myself.

Chapter 23 —

OLD LADY

They used to call me Old Lady. Although I did not think I would live long enough to get there, it was befitting. I always seemed to be more comfortable hanging out with the old folks. They could understand a deep conversation, were kinder than the kids my age and more patient than the young adults. Yes, according to Mrs. Good and the lady across the street, I was an old soul who had already formed vast opinions about the world I lived in. On top of that, they said I was as stubborn as a mule and sounded like a cow when I cried. Truthfully, I did not know what the mule and cow had to do with it but I thought being advanced in my years meant obtaining reverence. To me it represented the defining moment in your life when you and your words would be respected.

Trust me, I got excited over what that implied.

"Hakunna mattata" (without any worries or cares). I believed it to be a time when you knew everything, and a time when your children would wince at the idea of ever acting like you. The possibility was something I could only long for: a time I would be able to ponder, not be so serious all of the time, set aside being critical about my appearance, make jokes, and say what I wanted—when I wanted to say it.

Although I liked the image of my nickname, my peers were horrified about becoming old. We had two different points of view. While I always cherished the wisdom and confidence of the old, they saw their grandparents and elderly neighbors being mistreated and abandoned. They had no connection with old people, thought they were complacent, and decided the Golden Years would be different for them. I could actually picture how they imagined it:

> You had an antiquated look and were
> wearing wrinkles. You had no muscle
> tone and the hearing aid must have been
> turned down—because you just kept
> shouting and repeating stories that you
> told me time and again.
>
> What happened to you? You were
> sporting a cane and walking the way
> that I did when I had an ankle sprain.

Your speech was a little slurred and your
hair and clothes were nothing I ever
imagined. Then I thought about all
we had done previously and the good
doctor said, "one day it might happen to
you."

He must be wrong to think I was buying
the, *you will be getting old song.*

———

YOU WILL BE OLD LIKE ME

It was hard to contemplate
how your mind had been of late
I recall saying,
"pull yourself together and concentrate"

While I promised never to get to that state
They said you did well,
considering your birth date

I am not independently wealthy
But I exercise and try to eat healthy

No "Crispy Creams" for me and my genes
Only lean meats, salads and beans

How could you ever have been like me
I have enough energy to hang free from a tree

Look at you, sitting around and drinking tea
Then reading books you can hardly see

Your hair is gray
And one task may take all day

You can hardly hear me
And your stories are dreams that can't be

What makes you think you ever knew a thing
The world is different now,
what could you possibly bring

There is no such thing as living too long
Those old people
must have done something wrong

When I came to visit you once again
I was trying to figure when that old thing began

As I watch you move in the depths of slowness
I know this life has no time for your oldness

I want to care, but is it fair
That you have actually become
a helpless nightmare

I know it should be a time for respect
But I happen to reside in an era
which condones neglect

I am sorry, but my time with you has to be brief
I can no longer watch you sport those false teeth

I finally hit the road
Convincing myself, you let yourself get old

It can't be that you were ever like me
Lifts, stiffs and technology, will save this pedigree

They say you were once worth your weight in gold
That's why I am putting a hold on ever getting old

YOU WILL BE OLD LIKE ME
In Memory of Agnes Light

I was told to live my life to the fullest because one day I would be old. It was supposed to scare me but it never did. Back in the day, being elderly meant that I did not return my father's pistol to the side of my head and pull the trigger myself. It meant I did not realize the results of my action and I made it out of that maze: where the turns in life were confusing, the roads were shorter and the holes in the grounds were dug much deeper.

For me, there was so much more to being old; in all of my naivety, I figured God would simply forgive the ripened person—for all of the mistakes that they were tired of making. While the other children played, I sat there on the white marbled step with the elderly lady next door. Day-in and day-out, Ms. Agnes and I watched the block. She always seemed to be able to see what blinded me and there was always something to be learned. The old woman would point out the good and the bad and if there was none of that, we would just sit and enjoy the absolute silence, which appeared to be a waste of time to those keeping an eye on us.

I could not imagine the harm in it, but Mother had a problem with a child being satisfied with just sitting there with an elderly lady. The influence was something she did not want but something that I appreciated. Besides, what would I have been doing if the old woman were not there? She intrigued me with her wisdom and her game of surprises. She would leak out short bits about her past, make me aware of what she had learned from it and then shut down on the rest of the story. She was the best of Paul Harvey and the illusion and knowledge in a proverb. She was the beginning of the "Don't ask, don't tell policy" and trust me, I never asked the woman about her years on the block.

Two-V and I were taking piano lessons. One day after practicing, Ms. Agnes got up from a chair, sat on the wooden piano bench and just started playing. The old woman never mentioned this talent but there she was making notes stand up on their toes in a pirouette. Her hands were going and her head was tilted to cool. One knee was flashing itself by going up and down and then just like that, she blew the house down with her old timer's Rhythm and Blues. I stood back with my mouth opened and I reacted in a sign language that meant BRAVO! I never heard Ms. Agnes play again but believe me, there would be more days of enlightenment.

As she sat around in an old frumpy dress, I heard about the delicacy of snake meat, which I thought was a game to entrap fools. You should have seen me carrying that childhood knowledge. "Yea right, you ate that! Ok, you really think I am dumb enough to fall for that one." Just when I was getting smarter, I learned that every unresponsive person was not necessarily dead. Sister was passed out cold on the couch. My two younger sisters and I tried to wake her—but there was no response. We lifted her arm straight up and it fell faster, heavier and harder than we expected. I pinched her, pulled her feet, lifted her eyelids and screamed in her ears. When nothing worked, Two-V and I went into a panic and started to weep. Three-K, who always knew what to do in an emergency, ran out of the house to get the old woman.

As we were telling Ms. Agnes about the tragedy of impending doom, one loud snore came out of the top portion of Sister's mouth. Maybe we were wrong! Then the girl choked back a couple of swallows and just like before, her chest fell and there was dead silence. The old woman never touched Sister; she just looked at the teenager and without any further assessment she said, "She's drunk!" "Drunk!," we said—and the woman's head nodded in a single yes and walked out of the door at a slow smooth pace and acted as if nothing ever happened.

That elderly lady was full of surprises, especially when she stepped into the house with armor and stopped a father from beating his son. Dad was in a bad mood and he just kept beating and beating Big Brother. The man sat in a chair gripping a belt like a whip. Back and forth—and after a long period, he would pause, take another drink and start the show all over again. Mother was not there, so the woman took it upon herself to interfere. She stood tall, raised her voice and pierced the man with a look in her eyes that demanded he stop. She hexed him! As my father went into a state of paralysis, she took his car keys and drove my brother away.

Darn, the old woman put an end to another day of abuse and she could drive! All that time and I never knew she could peel out onto the road. I thought she had no other means of transportation, as she pushed her Acme brand shopping-cart to' and fro' her lucrative job at the Laundromat. Ms. Agnes was a hoot and I think the elderly woman knew me a lot more than anyone else. She analyzed my thoughts and knew when I was up to daring myself to do something outrageous. She knew I wanted to fit in but found a way to let me know: Those who committed that sin never won. Although the elderly lady realized I was a frightened child comforted by her strong character and her playfulness, she was ahead of any game that I was about to begin.

In years to follow, the thought of being old was always my answer to some kind of understanding—and always an improbability due to my mind's sterility. I combed through the thickness of the maze, and the byways told me that I was lost in a temporary place where I would not live long enough to get through it. Ms. Agnes said I was being released from the comforts of my womb and she understood why it was hot for me on cold days and rainy when the sun was shining. As pressure transmitted a fluid medium, I was lonely in a full room while my blood ran like a faucet and funneled like a typhoon. I think the elderly lady knew what was happening to me because she could see past the eyes of that child and peer into the belly of this woman.

Was I depressed? I was not sure. I just did not want outsiders to put a name on what I was feeling. I did not want them to saturate the thinking side of me with chemicals. I was sure they were drugs that would attach to the very area of my brain—which helped me recognize exactly where I was. I could not come up with the right word for what I was feeling on the inside. So I consulted my Allies and they suggested the feeling was only me, stepping past my own shadow, making an analysis of where I was in the maze, and noting where I needed to turn to get out of it.

About a year later, I saw the signs of a full life and tried to keep the discovery of it to myself. I relished how it was standing there in the perfect spot, waiting for me to notice its' rising. I stared at it for some time and when I finally put my fingers there, the texture was very different.

Yes, it had me written all over it. A gray hair! I was sure none of the other kids had one of those. I thought to myself, "This has to mean something," and from then on gray hair was symbolic for me. It was between white and black, and represented a distinguishing condition of truth, comfort and understanding. It came prematurely but it was a centerpiece for my estimates and guesstimates about the length of my life, as I was invited to come to terms with myself.

I did not want anyone to know what I found. So I pulled the treasure out and only showed it to the old woman. She did not know why I was fancying a strand of gray hair, but told me that I would have *two* of those beauties the next time they grew in. I grinned from ear to ear and must admit, when that thing popped out of my head—I could not help but love it.

Anyway, I counted fifteen gray hairs today and hope you can fathom this memory. As I go on to another chapter in my life, I finally found a way to write myself a letter. A friend asked me, "If you were eighty-years-old, what advice would you give yourself right now?" Initially, I could not get that far ahead of myself, but stick around. It is amazing what a few gray hairs can do!

Chapter 24 —

FROM FUTURE TO PRESENT

You know, I like the idea of writing on two-ply. I cannot rip out what I do not like; and what I do like breaks down easier and faster. Loose-leaf is uncomfortable. In dry conditions it can last years and leave a trail that exposes those secrets which are imprinted within my life and your life. It can be a scary thought, especially when you see people on those television shows running to their shredders. As they show reenactments, they say those things really happened. Then there is a commercial break and you go to sit on the pot. It is a moment to think and a time when you can flush super absorbent bathroom tissues without anyone ever suspecting that they had become your diary. I write the naked truth on 4.5 by 4.5—and the question is, "If I do not flush the whole thing, how long will it withstand the wear and tear of time?" Let's move on to the letter that I was encouraged to write—a letter from my future self to my present being, a letter initially written on two-ply.

> I am the elderly woman sitting to the right of you. My hair is short and a natural salt and pepper color. I have some wrinkles in my face but the locals say I look a lot younger than my years. As I put on my lipstick, I make outdated jokes and still watch those football players make tackles; they ruffle my feathers and make me giddy. I say "crunch!" and the old dog next to me cowers and flashes a look indicating I am just a little bit much for him.
>
> I still have lots of zest and when those basketball players get down on defense and climb over my head to dunk it, I scream out "Homerun!" What a glare—the grandpas in the family room think I am confused. They look at each other in unison and say: "Darling that is another game." Laughing out loud, I just wink at them through my rose colored glasses, tread a refined woman's pace and whisper to them: "Sweethearts, that's what you think!"

Most people my age are forgetful and
retired, and they do not know how
to have fun. While they moan and
groan about the aches and pains they're
having, I just ingest my cod-liver-oil,
put a little heat on my withering limbs
and start my engine. There is no stalling
here. I spend lots of time in the business
I started and insist on keeping people
my age in a certain frame of mind: "No
matter what, you should be living."
Although, everyone is tired of seeing the
aged woman in their face, they laugh at
her humor and watch the baby boomer
set aside those miniscule hearing aids
and ride the roller coaster to the edge of
grace.

I love my life now. There are new
metaphors and the past leaders are now
"Generation Next" hip-hoppers who
take Shuttle America to their vacation
homes on Mars. Communication is
astounding. I dial up my Face Phone,
put in my voice prompt and there you
are talking to me in your out of date
Jumex Shirt. I give you a heads up on
the new Congress and then I blink you
off so that I can get to the Century Store
to buy devices to compensate for my
impaired vision.

I still like to write and as I start my letter to my younger self, I tell her not to pull the trigger. I tell her to unload the barreled weapon and give herself a chance to be right here with me. I say, "Honey, this is from me to you."

It seems to be a long road to here but you can make it. I am not saying that you have to do it alone, so hold out your hand and trust again! Look at all that you have done thus far and realize how much further you could go if you dealt with yourself now. You know should have(s) and could have(s) are not good enough for you. So get in line with your inner spirit and listen to what I am saying.

It is a daily walk and as you analyze both your voluntary and involuntary movements, I know what you are feeling. You are not as dumb as you once thought you were and you are a lot more prepared than you think. Look at yourself and take your own advice. Believe in a sound mind and follow-up on an exciting stimulus. Stop telling yourself you have done what you wanted to do and make moves to do what you really know you should be doing.

When you are on the tightrope, place your footing carefully and find your balance. Do not step on people and do not stop treating them the way you always have. Just for once, stop letting them take advantage of your kindness and take a stand. Let them know when they have insulted you and then move past their tensions and into the shadows of God's miracles.

Stop running from this life of influences and do what is right for you. Do not stop looking at the person that captures your eye and peaks your attention. If that is the one who puts the wind in your sails and completes you, then go with it. There is no perfect guy and no perfect girl. Put your heart at ease and know when that special someone comes along, it is ok to take their hand.

I love you and would not mislead you. Stop thinking that Mr. Friend stole something you wish you had not lost. He took advantage of a child and you must understand that those feelings you experienced with other kisses has nothing to do with who you have become. That chapter in your life was written a long time ago and it is time to understand that you have already rewritten it.

Is life fair in a place where there seems
to be more hopelessness than hope?
Absolutely Yes! Every one of us has
struggles and would like to accrue
more good days than bad. Beyond our
shortcomings, we are all in a near life
experience, which makes living hard but
fair.

My love, stop inviting a near death
experience. Try to give of yourself—to
make the world a better place. You
will not save the planet but you will be
the light breeze that is blowing itself
on me. You will be the spirit that puts
forth an effort and you will be the eyes
in me that notify the weary, "Cacti are
blooming." People will hear through you
that the bees are buzzing and the birds
are making a special kind of music in
the trees.

You will be with your grandchildren
and they will describe you as a flower
standing with respect. They will say that
you loved drawing attention to them,
always encouraged them to devour
powerful words and insisted they try
harder. They will see you still looking
at their butts and then spinning them
around to let them know—you are wise
to what is really going on.

They will always be yours—and you
tell them to laugh with all of their soul
and to believe they are deserving of
the blessings that are revealed in their
talents. You instill in them that they are
the true lords of their land and all they
have to do is find a way to walk, lead,
love, witness and care.

We all can reap from the freshness of
the gardens in our soil. The vegetables
and fruits come and go in good crops
and in bad. Everything is authentic and
as we taste the something that came
from nothing, we hold on to a spirit that
fantasizes about the possibilities of self.

We all have mishaps and relapses, so to
heck with responding quickly—take
the time you need to find that seed,
which is more than a thought. Plant it
and see what comes of it. Be it, make
the most of it and become a source of
nourishment.

Girl, you have definitely moved on—
and if you could imagine where I am
right now: "You would live your dreams
in every aging day."

I gather this is the bulk of advice the future would give to the present. If I believe in her and listen to what she says right now, maybe it will keep us both out of harm's way. Perhaps if I look long enough, I will catch glimpses of her winking at me. Conceivably, I will hear her instilling pride and finding a way to be at my side.

Cadence: "Put your chin up, shoulders back and hips from side to side!" Who wants to miss the joys of living? On those days when the blues are steadfast and trying to put the pilot light to my spirit out, I want to gather my internal resources and rally my burning desires. I know that I will be the one who makes contributions that are useful!

I will hold onto my letter. Who knows, one day I may get a kick out of reading it to my much older self.

Chapter 25 —

CASTING CALL

I went to work last night and must tell you, the best part was getting off. I had not heard your voice during the long hours of darkness but there you were on the answering machine. I could not erase the message and every time I thought about talking to you, I had to stop myself from calling. I am sure it was much too early, so I put the key in the ignition and started to drive home. I thought to myself, "I really like this person but my feelings seem to go unnoticed."

I wanted more than a friendship. So the fantasy side of me began to audition my thoughts: The winner would one day stand up and tell the man exactly how I felt. One by one, each proposal went for a *casting call*. Some applicants stood out, others were exaggerated or nervous and some were never intended to make it to the stage.

> First Up: "We are so different from
> one another that when we come face to
> face again, you may not feel the way I
> do." Fired! That performance gets two
> thumbs down. The monologue is so
> mundane that I immediately kick it out
> of the script."

> Try Again: "Although I may appear to
> be awkward, this moment with you feels
> perfectly comfortable. It is quiet out
> there but inside here with you, it seems
> like I will never run out of words. You
> know I tend to get myself in trouble
> because:

—————

I have nothing on but WORDS—they are all I own

.

Words are rough and smooth and
They have a hidden rhythm that
Makes you sweat from their agenda

.

As salty water drips down past your eyelids
in a slow motion
Words allow you to read them and wander off
Into a space that is all your own

.

You make them what you want them to be

.

As you catch yourself sinking deeper
into a stimulating emotion
The words eventually come together in a
penetration
That makes you feel better by the moment
instead of by the day

.

You are filled up with the passion that is writing in you

.

There is a fast to slow pulsation
That rocks you like a heartbeat
But must be settled down before gaining control

.

When the words are powerful like this

.

Everything that ails you goes away
And everything is okay
Until you stop inscribing

.

When I stop, I search for more WORDS—
they are all I own

.

Sometimes I want to peel the clothes off of them
Sit in the dark with them
And make them create something
in the stillness of a quiet moment

.

I want them to be free

.

I want them to get down to the naked truth

> *And I want them to stretch out with meaning*
> *And live as long as eternity*

WORDS ARE ALL I OWN

Words are all I own and the only way I
know how to tell you exactly what I feel;
I like you and I wish I could hold your
heart a thousand different ways."

The director and theatrical producer said "Excellent."
They liked the thoughts that I had put together and will
allow me a *side.*

"Maybe I am just infatuated and
allowing my heart to lead. Perhaps I
am being very silly because it does not
make any sense to love you already. It
would be throwing caution to the wind
to tell you that I am fond of you; and
quite premature to say I feel a warm and
personal attachment."

Fantasy is so extravagant—and during the second
read they wanted wailing. I then caused tears to welter in
my eyes and cried out about the foolishness in my heart. I
then concluded and realized how life itself is a production
that each individual participates in. Additionally, if you are
living, you can not hide from life's dramatic gestures.

Well, according to my agent, I will have to wait for what happens next. I then grab my head and remember this is a casting call, where getting a person's attention is sometimes a profound hit—while other times it is a clear rejection. My chance is fifty-fifty. And, as I wait for the call, I wonder if I will finally be noticed in the crowd.

I could hear the phone ringing in the background. At first it startled me; but then I snickered at being in two places at once. I set my sights on reaching down to answer but the traffic was moving too fast. I was hoping the caller would leave a message; but then I thought, maybe I should attempt to answer. It might be the *casting call*—and I really want the part.

Chapter 26 ——

CRAVINGS

Time seems to be passing very quickly. The days are short and the nights are long. After working several night shifts in a row, I am starting my well deserved four days off and trying to convert back to being a day person. Suddenly, there I was in the mood for a dessert. There was nothing toothless in the house, so I drove over to the market. For fifteen minutes I walked up and down the snack aisle but nothing was fitting the bill. I told myself, "There has to be something in this store that could settle a craving."

This was the only place open at 2:00A.M. and I was not leaving until I could go into the "hereafter" with something that tasted like a Maple Cream Candy, a serious Baklava or maybe a Chocolate Éclair. I thought, "I better get a cart." The trip was taking too long and I needed something to lean on. As the desire was intensifying, I felt light headed and questionably deranged.

I traveled through Texas, Colorado, Okinawa, Utah, Korea, and Massachusetts. I took hops on those C3's and flew around the world. I drove on the Autobahn and after going as fast as I could, I made a pit stop to become a scholar. Then I was on vacation in an extraordinary place called Grenada, where the boys jumped off their island-made boats to catch the tourist coins. I did fall capture to spices and one islander's serenade. But then I saw my first Divi-Divi Tree in Aruba and was impressed with the chief goddess and a desert in the middle of the sea. While there, I met a man who let me feed his collection of exotic birds. They were the most beautiful collection I had ever seen. Then I continued on my journey to Venezuela and realized there were two very different parts, with one presiding in danger. Some houses were built on mud in a mountainous ravine that reminded me of the cardboard houses in the Philippines. Who would think I would ever see the same travesty.

At that point, I had to stop in Guadalupe because the world was all over me. I needed something sweet right away but did not realize the glucose in my blood was dangerously low and causing a hypoglycemic attack. I did not get to tell you about Hawaii or Puerto Rico but I must have been the only customer in that store—who had something coming over them.

All of those carts were perfectly aligned and there I was trying to untangle just one of the heavy two-wheeled vehicles from the bin. It was bad timing and I had no other choice but to kick the bottom wheel with my foot. Bang!—I popped something that freed all the buggies. Every single one of them launched in a different direction, causing unwanted attention that would make anyone feel like a found needle in a haystack. Someone called out, "are you OK?" "I am now," I said and I headed in the opposite direction.

Here we go again. "Maybe the pastry aisle will be more suitable." I stared through the glass case at a day's leftovers and suddenly, looking was not good enough. I bit into a Chocolate Éclair but the dough was a little too crunchy; it went into the cart. I found a Fudge Granola Brownie, which was dressed magnificently in powdered sugar. It was providing a little relief but it also landed in the metal basket.

After trying Ben and Jerry's Chubby Hubby Ice Cream, or something like that, and devouring some Pecan Sandies, a Mocha Log and a Walnut Finger, the checkout man walked up to me and wanted to know if he could help me find something. I batted an eye away from the opened peanut butter jar and replied, "As a matter-of-fact, you can." I told him I needed something sweet that was not already in my basket. The guy was very professional, he gasped as the peanut butter landed and asked me if I had something special in mind. "OH YES!

I would like a perfect Baklava with some cold milk!" He looked at me as if I were Forrest Gump and told me he would be right back.

"After all that—and all I had to do was ask." I wiped icing off my face and shook crumbs from my shirt. I did not want to look like some sort of slob; so I reached into my bag to get some Kleenex. Oh no—it was not where it usually was and neither was anything else! In a panic, I turned my purse upside down. My cash and credit card were left at home and a cool wetness covered my forehead; I was terrified.

I could not think fast enough, and there they were at 4:00A.M.—asking me about the taste sensation that was about to get me incarcerated. "I am sorry Ms., but we do not carry Baklava." The words that came out in the midst of me trying to figure out what I was going to do surprised me. "Well just forget about it!" I had no idea who I was going to call in Amish Country? The people at the hospital hardly knew me, my family was two hours away and I didn't even have my driver's license.

This was bad, so I decided to gather my thoughts and tell those guys that I needed to talk to the manager. The one to the left stepped a little closer to me and said, "I am the manager Ma'am. How can I help you?" We both stared into my basket of opened goodies and I told the gentleman that I had a problem. I relayed the gist of the story and asked if I could leave my name and address, and return in good faith. What a nightmare! We made our way to the customer service counter and of course there was a security guard right there. I did not expect him to say a thing, but he insisted on telling me why it was not good policy to eat anything in the store until it was paid for. What could I say? He was right and I was wrong!

The manager was awfully nice. He headed inside the office to get a pen and paper while Mr. Security gave me a few more pointers. I tried to interrupt the superhero—to tell him I remembered having a full can of spare change in my trunk, and to say I was nauseated. He put one finger up, signaling not to break in, and that was *all she wrote.* His black patent-leather shoes were covered with something that was indescribable. It was too late and jumping back did not stop those creased pants from receiving my stomach contents.

I could not lift my head, but the manager caught the tail end of our interaction and bellowed like I made his day. Mr. Security was totally disgusted and the manager was demanding someone get a mop, bucket and some paper towels. I heard the call for cleanup at the customer service counter and I was outdone. I was apologizing— while the boss was trying to reassure me that everything was going to be all right. He said the guard deserved what he got and said he understood because he had a pregnant wife who dismantled their kitchen trying to satisfy her cravings. I was not about to tell the man *"that is not my problem!"*

I needed to get out of there! I wanted to forget about the horrifying experience and insisted on paying my debt in quarters, dimes and pennies. It took forever but counting coins was no problem—especially after that "badge" just asked how he was supposed to believe who I was when I had no identification on me. I am definitely about obeying the law and do not plan to ever be unscrupulous at my neighborhood friendly grocery store again.

I am "cell-phobic" and there is nothing more sobering than remembering those days when I worked in Fulton County Prison. The prisoners sat in uncomfortable metal chairs, and without any emotion they told me about their innocence in the presence of doubt. I wanted to cry for them because it seemed like: *They did not have the intellectual capacity to understand—they were selling their liberty and returning to a system that was meant to keep them in a struggle.* In my analysis, they would be just as lost as those taken away from their homelands. They would be shackled with irons, branded and sure to miss certain opportunities before finding themselves again.

Don't worry: I will abide by the law, and there will be no enslaving or experimentation with those stale bologna sandwiches. The next time I get a craving, I will make sure the food I eat in that desperate moment—is already paid for.

Chapter 27

GIRL TALK

Gosh, I have been so busy that I almost forgot to tell you what I do and what happened when I first got here. As you know, Two-V was in trouble and I needed to be at her side and home with my family. Thankfully, I was able to take a leave of absence and signed a short-term contract for a travel assignment as a nurse in Lancaster Pennsylvania. Whoa! I was stuck in traffic behind a horse and buggy and was immediately aware that Lancaster was different. In some areas it seemed separated from the world I had known. In other areas it was just like any other county. The Amish people kept life simple and were known to examine change before they made it. They cooked food using fresh ingredients and seemed to be a hard working people.

"Getty up!" And on my nights off, I spent most of my time with Two-V who was a patient in another hospital that was two hours away. I guess many people wrote her off. She was laid up with a big bandage around her head. She had surgery more than once and when one of her skull bones became infected, they took it out. Two-V would not have liked the fashion statement she was making. She looked like a mummy with half a head. When it was time for her dressing changes, I tried to fill in the empty side with extra gauze, knowing she would be alarmed if she saw it.

The day came when I was finally allowed to bathe her. I managed to get her in the wheelchair and she must have slapped at me several times before we got to the door of the shower. The girl could not support any of her weight. I pivoted her onto the stool and underestimated how heavy she was. I started wheezing; the girl had already worn me out.

My sister was speechless. Wait! I mean she had not talked for a long time. Maybe there was a word or two, but when I turned on the water she started laughing. I was getting soaked and out of nowhere there was suddenly a waterfall of garbled words. I was elated, and as I kept working the words started making sense. She was talking about doing something to her doctor's toes. Listening intently, I thought it was so good to hear her talk! But then, she started getting into details that included this guy in a wheelchair. I said "What?" Oh no, "You need to stop!"

I was roaring at everything that Two-V was saying. Then she started telling me about this quadriplegic who was more vertical than the statue of liberty. You should have heard the girl scream with laughter. The stories got both of us going and I just pushed her to the inside of the bench and sat beside her. My hair went from straight to kinky and we both needed the hot water to run cold. We must have been making lots of noise. The nursing tech came in to check on us and we just stared at him and his feet. He was short but he must have worn a size thirteen shoe. Again, we started giggling. Then I asked the guy his shoe size. He got a real stunned look on his face and practically ran out of the room.

We were soaked, and it was time for us to come back to our senses. Then, I was sure Two-V's long term memory was intact. She said our parents had a great time making us and said something about them putting a padlock on their bedroom door. I told Two-V that I did not know anything about that, until I snuck into their room to see my little baby brother. I refuse to get into detail, but I got caught-up in an earthquake while I was hiding under their bed. I did get out of that space alive and knew I would not make the same mistake twice.

Our parents would have been shocked if they had heard us talking about subjects they were not prepared to discuss. They were divorced for quite some time and were trying to get use to being in the same room. Two-V was talking nonstop and I was starting to worry that one of my parents might be on their way to visit. Then I found a way to change the subject. I asked Two-V if she was hungry, then told her to concentrate and help me to get her back in bed.

Quieting down, the girl did everything she could to help me. As soon as her head hit the pillow, her eyes were closed and the room was as quiet as it had been when I arrived. What a good time that was. I dried myself off and proceeded to find some of Two-V's pajamas. I went with what was available, put on my hat, gloves, and winter coat, and left for home.

You know, that was the first time I ever had *girl-talk* with my sister. Although it was one of my most memorable moments, I knew there was a ninety-nine percent chance—the girl would not remember one of our best days together. Still, I was not about to let anything bring sadness to me. I would remember what happened for both of us, and now I was more inspired to put my words down on paper and keep them there.

The next day, when my mother came, Two-V asked for Chinese food about ten times. She demanded "Vegetable Lo Mein" and only wanted it from a specific place. This was a very good sign, but even more significant when the Chinese Doctor came into the room to examine her. Two-V started telling "the whole truth and nothing but the truth." Her inhibitions were gone, as she said things that were startling enough to land on the first page of the National Enquirer. The doctor explained it was normal, but Mother was embarrassed when her daughter started talking intimately about the good doctor's toes. It was a lot to comprehend but I finally understood that Two-V had to let go of anything that was standing in the way of her recovery.

Chapter 28 —

SIFTING

It is phenomenal when you realize what a miracle really is! As I am examining myself carefully, it seems to me that certain inaccuracies, misunderstandings and disputes have less importance. In fact, when you watch someone walking the tight-rope between life and death, you might go through a growth process that leaves you using words like "trivial" or "silly" to describe quarrels and differences that you had in the past.

Once I focused on what was truly important, I passed through a fine sieve. All of the stress and extra baggage left behind in the straining device was nothing but drama. In my new state of mind, I looked back and wanted to remember everyone who deserved an apology from me. I wanted to throw out the debris, go around the world and make amends. As my heart stepped into a new day, I was open to a two-sided edge of forgiveness. I was thinking, "It really is give and take along with forgive and be forgiven." Yes, I stood in this world sifting through the wreckage of my mistakes, only to recognize— the affected person's bitterness and anger became my pain and most likely your pain too. I tried to avoid being evasive because when I asked myself "Why?" I am not sure I handled some issues in the best way. Then, regardless of what I comprehend right now, I lived with the outcomes.

I sifted some more and noticed: When my burdens were great, I spent an unusual amount of time in my car. I also slept less and dreamed more. Well, unknown to me, driving until I was weary was all a part of my sifting process. I was thinking and then dozing. This was followed by swerving in the dangers of the road. Year after year I told myself to pull over; I said, "I won't do that again" and then woke up the next day with pieces of me closer together instead of further apart. Thank goodness I started writing again; regret would not have been able to bring back the unfortunate person(s), lying in the wreckage.

Now that I am back on the East Coast, I think about how different my life is on the West Coast. In a moment I am over my past. But then, I feel the tension in the pit of my stomach. I think, "Maybe I need to come to terms with myself so I don't just show up in the shadows of a tragedy." Lots of people do that—and it puzzles me why we wait for a funeral to put our differences aside and come together. Why is there always "no time," only to be put in a situation where you have to "take the time?"

I guess these are the types of things we ask when it is too late. Surely we could do better if we tried. Who knows what that entails for you, I know I cannot always do it on my own strength. Like it or not, I do need someone else to help me when it comes to reconciling with those things that have left a bad taste in my mouth. That's why I think it is imperative to take steps to understand your heart and your fear. I know I have not found all of the answers, but I am sitting here looking at someone—in a place that any-one-of-us could be in.

When I think about the processes that Two-V had to go through to get to this point in her recovery; I realize the difference in how I thought about her situation <u>then</u>, verses how I think about it <u>now</u>. The doctor said Two-V still had some brain activity; *I am asking God to let the girl tell us her last wishes.* I thought the girl was going to die; *you should see Two-V taking her life back.* I just wanted to hear the girl talk too much one more time; *Two-V says she can't remember anything.* I just wanted to tell my sister that I accepted who she was and that I loved her; *Two-V is awake and says she loves me too.*

Day in and day out, I thought about everything. I was waking my own self up, working my way through that eighty year old woman's words and trying to take my own advice. I did not have to audition to be myself. I did not have to wait so long to satisfy my cravings. I was the past, the present and the future—and already who I was meant to be. Yes, it took some sifting to come to this. But just as my breath was taken away in the most erotic dance, it was given back to me and I knew exactly where my heart belonged. I could not start my life over because I lived with everything I had ever done. So I laid back and let the electrical impulse take over at a slower propulsive pace. It felt wonderful to grow and realize—I was getting rid of so much baggage.

Weighing less, I now choose what makes me a better individual. I choose the one that loves me at my best and worst. I choose the one who sees me on the inside and wants to be with me anyway. I choose to try a little harder. I choose to show up at my loved one's door-step just to say hello. It is not too late to come to terms: to say I am sorry, ask for forgiveness, or say I forgive you. So what if I do not get the response that I would like! It is not always getting what I want that counts. It is me turning my insides out, walking away with graciousness and coming together with elegance and respect.

I know that many people think it is a bunch of malarkey, but on my worst days, it was the warm courtesies and compassion that gave me hope for myself and the rest of the world. Imagine what it would be like if everyone just tried a little harder to give and receive kindness, to encourage someone to give their best and to tell them they can make it to the finish line.

I was not dreaming this time. I was breathing the life within me. As I kept trying to understand why I was not the one with an embolus in my head, I sought to know and understand me. How much more sifting did I have to do? Then, I asked myself "Who are you anyway?"

Chapter 29 —

THE TRUTH

Who am I anyway? I am expression, love, complication and so much more. At times I look way too serious but my smile separates the heavens from the earth. I am you—and regardless of age, sex, religion and origin, I am just another part of this beautiful mystical creation, looking at my potential errors and striving for continuous improvement.

The truth is: I am somebody, I have a purpose and I have a reason to be here. When I sort through the delicacy of my hibernating thoughts, I suddenly know that no one is better than me, because they are me! They are the guaranteed stages in my life, classified as: newborn, infant, child, adolescent and adult. Yes, I know who I am

now and realize why I can't let someone else say they
know me—when they really do not know me at all.

> Deceased—and you are the only one left
> to say who I was. As I am being laid to
> rest, you insist on sharing the memories
> of who you think I was. Your words
> avoid my controversies, drown on bits
> of heresy, and give the crowd pieces of a
> false legacy.

> I am the only dead person lying there
> and you are the contradictory speaker
> who is exaggerating and reminding
> me that two and two can equal more
> than four. I heard you say, *"**Reticent**
> was straight and outspoken."* I listened
> to your individual perception of loss
> and watched you skip over **Demon's**
> insecurities and prickly outbursts. You
> mentioned **Wit's** confidence, harped on
> one dimension in Creativity and ended
> with the social functions of **Personality.**

> From the grave, I heard myself scream
> out, "Tell the people the truth!" Rolling
> around: I said, "Don't you know my
> Allies, don't you know **Me**? Come on,
> those are not my last words. Get it
> right!"

Most of us do care what people say about us. I am a seeker who never trusted enough to tell anyone who I am. I wear a brown color on my skin and it is true—some people make assumptions before ever speaking to me. It does not matter what mix of blood I have in me, I was assigned one race, one nationality and one social security number. Then I was told how far I might go and how I would someday use 1619 to 1860 as a current reason to indulge in failure and self-pity.

Indeed, slavery in the roots of my history does impact the playing field. And yes, some people do get stuck right there in the middle of preconceived judgments. Then they take a detour and get lost on some side road. Sorry, "I can't do that." If that road block presents itself, I am going straight through it. As expected, I will get thrown around, pick up some dents and may even get ejected. But where would I be if I did not discover how to make something out of nothing? Who would I be if I did not experience my life just the way it is? What would I be if I never took time to discover my own flavors? How would I have learned the totality of my worth, if I never fought for it?

I am loneliness in the heart of an unproductive day. I am humbleness at the end of a hard lesson. I am just like everyone who ever looked back in the mirror and saw how they almost gave up on everything. I am the one who needed to hear those simplistic words being uttered to me, "You can." It did not matter where the encouragement came from (family, friend, counselor, minister, teacher, mentor, doctor, psychic or intuition); because eventually, I had to be the one who said "I believe in me and I will make use of the talents I have." I had to be the one to break through the barriers that were holding me back.

Although I am here with you now, how many times do you think I said that I was committed to doing everything that I could to the best of my ability? Then I would feel the bump in the road and oops—my desire was gone. At first, there was no way for me to write this chapter. There were too many secrets in the way and a lot of bumps that I let get the best of me. In actuality, it is easier to give up and much harder to hold our heads up and say we tried. Some of us really can not handle the truth about our failure, attitude, disability, sexuality, job description, so-on and so-forth. It is not pleasant being rejected, uncomfortable to accept criticism and difficult to change. We feel defeated, go on to the next best thing, and again on to the next best thing—never finishing anything. Now that I have made another effort to keep my words right here, I have so much more to share with you.

Telling you the truth, I have not figured out where I will be forever; but I am me, and not necessarily what you want me to be. I admit to being a dreamer, but I am certain dreams do come true. As I took walks through the uncultivated desert and said hello every time I came upon a new idea, I thought I was free:

But apparently I asked the wrong
questions at home, school, and work.
I looked things up and researched
information before they sent me off to
find answers that were not there.

What is so wrong with saying that you
don't know? Why not answer a question
truthfully in a high-powered meeting?
Why dance around the issues and lose
the point you are trying to make? It is a
strange situation and an awkward place
to be when those around you cannot
leave the debate where it belongs. They
get carried away, take it home, bring
it into your friendship and make it
personal. We will not always agree but
why do people say "It is over" when it
really isn't?

Mother says, "There is a right and a
wrong way to talk to someone." Does
that mean you should lie to them or let
them misinterpret your goodness for
weakness? When someone says "No"
in a kind voice, how many times do
you think it will be taken for "Yes?"
How many institutions think they are
culturally diverse—just because they
met a quota? How often are you told
you are working for the best, only to
find out: They do not want to hear what
will make them better?

Despite all this, I thought I was
supposed to tell the truth. I endured
orientations and lectures learning how
to deal with the aspects of Human
Resources. Yet, just as I did as a child,
I needed to recruit more fiction than
fact. I needed to learn the game of
speaking in riddles and use words that
most people did not understand. I had
to calculate the best times to wear a
skirt instead of pants. I needed to only
tell the truth when those receiving it
were ready to hear it. I should have
patted people on the back, even if I was
about to fire them. I learned to turn the
other cheek but truthfully could not see
myself saying "If you do me a favor, I
will do the same for you."

So just like me, you tried and got yourself ejected!
How about this: Get off your butt, make some changes,
get back behind the wheel, try again, and be prepared
to knock down more barriers! In this system of things,
whether we like it or not, we take part in an ever changing
world and definitely have the right to believe our dreams
can come true. I am not telling you a lie—because we
also have the privilege to ignore our surroundings and get
lost in the beautiful iridescent tail feathers of a peafowl.

Once fanned by the bird's impressive show, abandon your internal authorities and say, "There is no bottom line." You might think you hear me asking you to say there are no limits or restrictions. OK, now imagine what you just said is, "I don't care, it does not matter to me, why bother with the truth, why help, why try, etc."

Then what? Zero—all of those public speakers and not one of them is willing to stand firm and tell the people the truth. Zip—not even your doctor has time to listen to the details of your illness. Zilch—he, she and they will tell you who they want you to be. Kaboom—why am I, my children, our parents, siblings, friends, neighbors and colleagues fighting another war?

Facts become reality and the truth wakes you up. So go ahead and fold up those truths and put them in the brim of your hat. While you are coming to terms with what it really means, know that I have traveled to many parts of the world. When I finally tasted life, there was the sweet and the sour. Everything is two sided and we are dichotomous pieces of existence making a personal journey. Agreeing to disagree, I scream that I am human, I do make a difference and I am alive.

> Wait! Did the speaker say I was deceased? No, that can't be! I am still hungry, my heart still wants to beat for me, and I just started telling you the truth.

Forget this! I am not ever taking on the
role of being a corpse again. You know,
I did not get that part I wanted in the
"Casting Call" so I am playing dead.

OH, I better break through this barrier
and speak up now. I know who I am, I
have something to offer and I have too
much unfinished business. I had better
try a little harder to let someone know I
am still in here. I certainly don't want
to get buried by mistake.

I grabbed onto my heart that was always wanting
to—and finally did something about it. Willingly, I took
your breath, traveled back and forth through my life, and
chose this moment to try living again. As I was clearly
resuscitated, I knew the truth. Love and inspiration were
always there for me.

———

Alert and oriented, then I closed my eyes
I started to dream;
they thought I was saying goodbye

They could not detect my heartbeat
Or wake me out of a perfect sleep

I was flying high as they were ready to cry
Family and friends on standby,
asking God "Why"

It was best for me, letting myself be free
Looking at the stages in my life—and me

I was sucking my teeth and enjoying a sweet
I saw them running to where my Allies and I meet

I must have forgotten about the date
As a taste of temptation made me late

There they were and the place was packed
Who is that slipping a board under my back

Hey, get out of my room right now
I was simply bearing down

You know, I was swallowing my treat
And here you come removing my sheet

Why are you pounding and bouncing on me
And sticking my arm with that Christmas Tree

Listen: I really am not the one to kiss
Especially with that head-tilt chin lift twist.

Please wait
Before you defibrillate

Cause I am concentrated high on O2
And getting ready to follow through

   "Shock! Shock! Shock!"

Realizing my action potential
Getting on track was essential

Inspiration was my friend
And there I was living again

Yes, as I hold my heart in my hand
I remember the words "I CAN "

RESUSCITATION
For Victoria

Chapter 30 —

ONE GRAIN OF DESERT SAND

They were encouraging words on a page: "Run Spot Run." At that moment, I was inspired to read, compelled to ask too many questions and wanted to learn my ABC's. I would get red-hot scrutinizing <u>Roots</u>; I became webbed in the tub reading suspicious novels; and I huddled-up under the covers reading <u>Jaws</u>. I liked the idea of it all—until it became a required text that taught me nothing about my own history and all about the voyages of Christopher Columbus and his discovery of the New World. I could not enjoy a hot dog or buttered popcorn reading those sorts of things, nor could I figure out why I needed information that did not help to land me anywhere but in a struggle with my parents.

I must have received a "D" in that class and only recovered when I got glimpses of the Civil War, which brought hints of freedom to a people who never would be free. Then I was learning about all who were enslaved: Africans, Native Americans, Irish, Jews, and many others. How could they have survived—if they did not have the foresight and curiosity to build into the heavens; the inspiration to break sound barriers; the encouragement to scour with arrows; and the motivation to run abroad in chains?

I was captivated and would one day discover what history was all about. It was our very own roots growing over time. Whether we accept it or not, we all have a place in history. While some would disagree with that point, the attraction remains: "Everything in this world is questionable, arguable and discoverable." For instance, I was taught that the most important point about Mr. Columbus was finding out this world was not flat. I was instructed to never move to California because it was going to fall into the ocean. I was encouraged to read Revelations because, ever since I can remember, this period of time was about "the last days."

No! Do not write this off or think that these sorts of things are not worth paying attention to. I have learned that everything in my mind is worthwhile—even if it only bears a second of wonder and a minute of retention. Do not laugh at those who are inspired to share something that makes no sense to you. Heed your sarcasm because the person telling the story could be you; it could be someone you know trying to describe how to make the perfect meal with a pinch of love and a dash of despair; or, it might be me writing a narrative and finally finishing it.

Inspiration has led me this far in my development and it holds a place for you. No matter how negative or positive, the result of inspiration puts new meaning to words that are sometimes: silent or loud, imagined or real, happy or sad, foretold or unpredictable. Words are wealth and I can not imagine a place without them. "Lubb-dubb," and words are strong and suspicious. As I read them, I wonder what is lurking between every line and inspiration makes me think ahead in search of the best conclusion.

As I started the long race, I inhaled and pictured myself crossing the finish line. When I visualized acknowledgements for reaching my goal, I saw myself giving a speech that I prepared on my last leg of thought.

THANK YOU ALL SO VERY
MUCH! I needed you to keep me going
and that is why I am happy to be here,
at the finish line with you. As I hold my
heart in my hand, who would ever think
I could have completed this run? Trials
and miles and regardless of the running
time, I succeeded in getting through the

agony and defeats of this marathon.

Thank you for making contributions to benefit those who have always wanted to and will finally do something about it. Thanks for helping me prepare for this and reminding me how good my life turned out to be. Mile by mile, I am not disappointed with turning onto the road that led me in this direction. Thanks for encouraging me to consume those ample carbohydrates and fluids responsible for preserving my strength along the way. Your belief in me and the sincerity of your character helped me to possess the best possible attitude—to stay in a race that has eluded me throughout my lifetime.

As I returned to the Southwest, I knew that I would never stop experimenting with the flavors within me. On the horizon, I saw an Oasis and understood the importance of one grain of desert sand.

———

A man stands tall before them and lends
his strength in times of need
Although he smiles and loves on good days,
he endures everyday

He is grateful for what he has now

191

And never takes for granted
what he may need later

Those who know him say
He bears the tribal marks
of his ancestors
Shows no fear in manipulating
his own interpretation
And does not hesitate
to make sacrifices for others

As the man's eyes are right
He strives to become better
He knows if he gives it his all,
he can be at ease
And allow his heart to beat on the left

Do you know this man
HE—IS—THE—ONE—WHO—SUCCEEDS

He crawls before he walks
and thinks before he speaks
He gains while he attains
and configures a way to maintain

Legacy says
As his bright star walks beside him
And stands with him
in the "Living Water"
He is the one who makes the difference

Do you know this man
HE—IS—ONE—GRAIN—OF—DESERT—SAND

ONE GRAIN OF DESERT SAND
For Pete

Chapter 31 —

INSPIRATION

I said in the beginning of this narrative that, "I was always wanting to follow through and complete something that I started but never finished." In my case, I have been trying for quite some time to leave my words on paper so I could write the dream. It seems like a simple task—but when I traveled back and forth through my life, everything changed.

You see, I was unbelievably gullible:

> The nice man sitting on the couch gave
> me red jellybeans. I saved them for later
> but as I pulled them out of my pocket
> to share, the lady who was getting a fix
> in the upper level of the boarded house
> stared at them, threw the drugs on the

ground, slapped my hands and told me
to never accept anything from a stranger
again.

Farther and farther away from people
and deeper and deeper into myself I
went. I watched movies and tried to
imagine my own plot. As my own
world scared me, I earned frequent flier
miles and traveled to nonexistent places.
In and out of reality, I slid slowly inside
to a safe place—that held secrets and
concealed my pain.

I am thinking that ninety-nine percent of the time,
people get in the way of themselves. We bury the pain
without resolving it and then we do not understand why
we can't get past the simple things. It is puzzling because
we somehow manage to get the tools we need to succeed,
but will avoid anything that reminds us of what we locked
away. We seem to have the desire to complete something,
but can not say what really stood in the way of us finishing
it.

I always wanted to write this book. After telling
myself I could not come up with another excuse for not
completing it, I carried paper and pencils everywhere I
went and called them my utensils. Determined to share
"A TASTE OF ME," I realized that what I had to say
might inspire others. You know, sometimes you want
to give back and help others but you can not make a

donation, give blood or do volunteer work. I remember one time during my graduate program; I was very ill and had to spend a couple of days in the hospital. It was almost graduation day and some students wanted to get a gift for the secretaries. I really did not have any money and was unable to contribute. I can tell you, it was humiliating to find my name on the email that listed me and two other people as "The Weakest Link." I don't know how the Dean was able to condone something like that, but I could hardly hold my head up on the day of my graduation ceremony. I am telling you, if I could have made something out of nothing on that very day, I would have.

So I became even more inspired to share something while I have the resources. Then, I told some of my friends that I was writing a story containing a half-cup of fact and a pound of fiction. The responses varied, but drew the most attention when I finally leaked the title. I was asked, "How do you get to name your book something like that?" Then, when I said "No, it is not a cookbook," their imaginations went a little farther than I expected! However, I was overjoyed when one of my readers called and said "Hey, I was inspired by your cookbook. It is unconventional nutrition that gives you energy to actually do the things that you always wanted to do."

As you know, food is a very important part of our lives. While it keeps you and me alive, it may also put a smile on our faces, make us anxious in anticipation of the next bite, or torment us with unbelievable cravings. In my case, food has always been right there with me. It was still there even when I ignored it. So why not include it in this piece? Every experience, idea and talent that you and I have are flavors that have the ability to stimulate an appetite. When I say, "We all have a story to tell," you may start to think about the ones that you have. You know—the ones that could scare a child straight, sober a person up or lay in the center of a plate demanding attention.

I hope that after reading this, you are aware that food is more than just nourishment. Now open your mind and imagine with me:

> As you gather all your _senses_, a
> gourmet meal is sitting at your center,
> encouraging you to eat it and get all
> that you need from it. I am writing the
> dream and I am certain you have to
> *touch* on the basics in life to enhance the
> end product. Once you *hear* the sizzle,
> know that I am putting forth my best
> effort. As I start to present "A TASTE
> OF ME," you should be able to *see* the
> inside story forming on the plate. The
> words are making you think. Whether
> you laugh, cry, or have any other
> emotion; recognize, the meal is going
> to be good for you. *Smell* the love that
> went into the recipe. As the aroma spills

into the air, know that hints of it are
being shared. Inspired all over again,
you pick up your utensils and begin to
taste an epicurean delight. As you are
eating, every chapter holds a different
flavor and message. Once every part of
you is involved and you have devoured
the powerful words—be inspired.

Savor "A TASTE OF ME." Those subtle flavors
become powerful words right before you swallow them.
There may be a hint of something; but if you attempt to
consume this cuisine too fast, it will surely be missed.
So slow down and enjoy every morsel! As you finish this
meal and sense a fullness of reflection and acceptance of
self, realize that you have the ability to accomplish more
than a dream.

Acknowledgments

Writing this book and having it published has been one of my greatest goals and accomplishments. I started out trying to do this by myself and soon found it to be bigger than I imagined.

With great pleasure I thank all the wonderful people who took their time and knowledge to help me get this book on the right track, especially to Oliver Tryba, Lisa Randall, Shari Overland, Anna O'Bannon, Alise Gerald and my cover designer Paolo Piro. Your critiques and editorial advice inspired me to complete this work.

Thanks to all of my friends out there who always seemed to lend a hand right when I needed it! Anna, Julie, Shari, Cynthia, Maria and Donna—you have been the friends that never turned your backs on my dreams.

Thanks to my family. You are all a part of my memories and I love you. Thanks Mom for continuously telling me to only say "I Can." You told me to take the words "I Can't" out of my vocabulary and that made a sound difference in my life. Shalamar, I finally got this done. Thank you for "Fire In The Sky."

Thanks to all of the nurses and doctors at the University of Pennsylvania Hospital Oncology Unit and the Philadelphia VA Hospital who helped take care of my sister Victoria. You were very patient and instrumental in helping with at least two miracles.

Thanks to my new friends in Lancaster Pennsylvania—especially to those who worked at Semper Care Hospital. You were one of the best teams I have worked with.

Finally, in memory of Alex, I loved your hugs and your innate ability to be true to yourself. You were the wine and the cheese and I will miss you.

Printed in the United States
70330LV00001B/1-9